Contents

Introduction

IGCSE Edexcel Mathematics A Practice Books 1 and 2 provide more material to enable the pupil to revisit topics prior to the examination. These questions will reinforce the basic principles whilst stretching and challenging the more able candidates. The chapters exactly match those in the Student Books and the same pattern of paired and graded exercises have been produced. Non-starred exercises are targeted up to and including grade B, whilst starred exercises are targeted at grades up to and including A*. There are four Examination Papers at the end of Practice Book 2 and all answers are available on www.pearsonis.com/edexceligcsemathsanswers.

advancing learning, changing lives

Edexcel IGCSE
Mathematics A

Practice Book 1

D A Turner, I A Potts

A PEARSON COMPANY

Published by Pearson Education Limited, a company incorporated in England and Wales, having its registered office at Edinburgh Gate, Harlow, Essex, CM20 2JE. Registered company number: 872828

www.pearsonschoolsandfecolleges.co.uk

Edexcel is a registered trade mark of Edexcel Limited

First published 2007
This edition published 2010 by Pearson Education Ltd.

14 13 12 11
10 9 8 7 6 5 4 3

ISBN 978 0 435 04416 9

Typeset by Tech-Set Ltd, Gateshead
Printed in the Malaysia, CTP-KHL

Number 1

Fractions, decimals, percentages, standard form (positive indices), directed number and rounding

Exercise 1

Write each of these as a fraction in its lowest terms.

1 $\frac{4}{12}$ **2** $\frac{4}{14}$ **3** $\frac{6}{30}$

4 $\frac{12}{96}$ **5** 0.5   **6** 0.25

7 0.2   **8** 0.75   **9** 0.1

10 0.3   **11** $2 \times \frac{3}{15}$ **12** $\frac{4}{32} \times 6$

Calculate these.

13 $5 \div 0.1$ **14** $12 \div 0.2$ **15** $3 \div 0.01$

16 $(-4) + 12$ **17** $(-4) - 12$ **18** $(-4) \times 12$

19 $(-4) \div 12$ **20** $(-4) \times (-12)$

Write the following percentages as fractions in their lowest terms.

21 25%   **22** 10%   **23** 75%

24 60%   **25** 35%

26 Find 10% of 1500 m.

27 Find 15% of $2400.

28 Increase 1500 m by 10%.

29 Decrease £2400 by 15%.

30 A mobile phone from Pineapple Net is advertised at a 25% reduction in the Christmas sales. Its price before Christmas is $120. What is the sale price?

31 Jermaine's pocket money is increased from €15 per week by 15%. How much does he receive per year after the increase?

32 Sami buys a computer game for £36 after the cost has been reduced by 36%. What was the original cost?

Calculate these, and write each answer in standard form.

33 $(3 \times 10^4) \times (2 \times 10^6)$ **34** $(8 \times 10^7) \div (2 \times 10^5)$ **35** $(7 \times 10^7) \times (8 \times 10^8)$

Write each of these correct to 3 significant figures.

36 1234   **37** 1235   **38** 1236

39 54321   **40** 54399

Write each of these correct to 3 decimal places.

41 1.2344   **42** 1.2345   **43** 1.2305

44 1.2035   **45** 1.2007

Exercise 1★

Write each of these as a fraction in its lowest terms.

1 $\dfrac{0.4}{4.4}$

2 $3.6 \times \dfrac{3}{72}$

3 $\dfrac{3}{70} \times 21$

4 $\dfrac{1.2}{3.2} \times \dfrac{2.4}{7.2}$

5 Find 10% of 5% of 8400 g.

6 Alec buys a model boat for £120, then sells it for £75. What is his percentage loss?

7 Mari buys a painting for €1250, then sells it for €1400. What is her percentage profit?

8 Jamal's fastest time for the 400 m is 70 seconds. In his next race he improves by 10% and in the race after that he improves from this time by 10% again.

    a What is his new fastest time?

    b What is his overall percentage improvement?

9 Ning was 1.25 m tall. One year later she was 10% taller and in the next year her height increased a further 12% from her new height.

    a What is her height after both increases?

    b What is her overall percentage height increase over the two years?

10 Umberto has a salary of €120 000. Calculate his new salary if it is

    a increased by 10% then decreased by 10%.

    b increased by x% then decreased by x%.

Calculate these.

11 $74.5 \div (0.1)^2$

12 74.5×0.001

13 $74.5 \div 0.001$

14 $74.5 \div (0.001)^2$

Calculate these and write each answer in standard form correct to 2 significant figures.

15 4321×1234

16 $(3.5 \times 10^8) \times (2.5 \times 10^6)$

17 $(3.6 \times 10^8) \div (7.2 \times 10^6)$

18 $(3.6 \times 10^8) + (7.2 \times 10^6)$

19 $(3.6 \times 10^8) - (7.2 \times 10^6)$

20 $(2.5 \times 10^5)^2$

Write each of these correct to 3 significant figures.

21 0.2005

22 0.002005

23 3075.7

24 47555

Write each of these as a decimal correct to 3 decimal places.

25 0.0785

26 0.0715

27 $\left(\dfrac{1}{4}\right)^2$

28 $\left(\dfrac{1}{3}\right)^2$

Algebra 1

Simplifying algebraic expressions and solving equations

Exercise 2

Simplify these as much as possible.

1 $2a + 3a$

2 $4x - x$

3 $6ab - 4ab$

4 $xy + 2xy$

5 $2a + 3b$

6 $4x + 4y$

7 $3xy + 4yx$

8 $5ba - 3ab$

9 $3x \times 2$

10 $5 \times 4y$

11 $2a \times 3b$

12 $5x \times 2y$

13 $4x \times x^2$

14 $3a^2 \times a$

15 $5a^2 \times 2a$

16 $2x^2 \times 3x^3$

Remove the brackets and simplify these if possible.

17 $4(x + y)$

18 $2(a + 2b)$

19 $3(a - b)$

20 $4(2x - y)$

21 $-2(x + y)$

22 $-3(a - b)$

23 $4 - 2(a + b)$

24 $5 - 4(x - y)$

Solve for x.

25 $x + 2 = 5$

26 $x + 5 = 2$

27 $x - 3 = 1$

28 $x - 7 = 3$

29 $4 - x = 2$

30 $7 - 2x = 3$

31 $2x = 10$

32 $4x = 12$

33 $\frac{x}{4} = 2$

34 $\frac{x}{3} = 2$

35 $\frac{4}{x} = 1$

36 $\frac{6}{x} = 3$

37 $2x + 3 = 5$

38 $3x + 8 = 2$

39 $3x - 4 = 2$

40 $4x - 3 = 9$

41 $3(x + 1) = 9$

42 $2(x + 3) = -10$

43 $2(x - 2) = 4$

44 $3(x + 4) = 6$

45 $2x + 1 = x + 3$

46 $4x + 2 = x + 14$

47 $3x - 2 = x + 4$

48 $5x - 4 = 2x + 5$

49 $4 - x = x + 2$

50 $1 - x = x + 7$

51 $2x + 3 = 12 - x$

52 $3x - 1 = 11 - x$

53 $7 - 3(x + 1) = 1$

54 $6 - 2(x - 1) = 2$

55 $x - 2(x + 2) = -5$

56 $4x - 3(x + 2) = 5$

57 $2(x + 3) - (x + 1) = 7$

58 $3(x - 2) - (x - 1) = 3$

59 $3(x + 2) - 2(x - 1) = 11$

60 $5(x + 1) - 3(x + 2) = 5$

Exercise 2★

Simplify these as much as possible.

1 $2ab + 3ba$ **2** $2xy + 2xz$ **3** $4xy - 2xz$

4 $3xy - xy$ **5** $4x + 3 - x$ **6** $5a + 5 + 5a$

7 $2y + 3z + y - z$ **8** $a + 6b - a + b$ **9** $2x \times 5y$

10 $3a \times 3b$ **11** $3x^2 \times 4x^3$ **12** $a^3 \times 7a^2$

13 $2x \times 4x \times 3x$ **14** $a \times 5a^2 \times a^3$ **15** $x^2 \times (2x)^2$

16 $(2a)^3 \times (3a)^2$

Remove the brackets and simplify these if possible.

17 $5(x + 2y)$ **18** $6(2a - b)$ **19** $3(2x - 5y)$

20 $4(3a + 4b)$ **21** $-4(x + y - z)$ **22** $-(2a + b - a)$

23 $6 - 3(x - y)$ **24** $8b - 2(a + b)$

Solve for x.

25 $x - 1 = 8$ **26** $3x - 1 = 14$

27 $x + 3 = 2$ **28** $2x + 9 = 5$

29 $8 - x = 10$ **30** $1 - 2x = 7$

31 $2x = 5$ **32** $3x = 4$

33 $\dfrac{x}{10} = 1$ **34** $\dfrac{x}{7} = 7$

35 $\dfrac{9}{x} = 3$ **36** $\dfrac{7}{x} = 7$

37 $5(x - 1) = 10$ **38** $3(x - 2) = -12$

39 $7(x + 2) = 21$ **40** $4(x + 3) = 8$

41 $2(x + 5) = 11$ **42** $3(x + \frac{1}{2}) = 6$

43 $3(x - 2) = 1$ **44** $5(x - 1) = 4$

45 $2x + 7 = 3x + 5$ **46** $5x + 6 = 2x + 3$

47 $5x - 4 = 2x + 8$ **48** $3x - 1 = 7x - 9$

49 $10 - 2x = 4 + x$ **50** $3 + 2x = 18 - 3x$

51 $5 - 3x = 7 - x$ **52** $2 - 4x = 1 - 5x$

53 $5(x + 2) - 3(x + 1) = 9$ **54** $2(x + 5) - (x + 4) = 8$

55 $3(x + 5) - 2(x - 1) = 19$ **56** $4(x + 2) - 5(x - 3) = 24$

57 $2(3x + 1) - 3(2x - 1) = 5$ **58** $5(2x + 3) - 3(4x - 1) = 12$

59 $4(x - 1) - 3(x + 1) = 2(x - 4)$ **60** $3(3x + 2) - 5(2x - 2) = 7(3x - 4)$

Graphs 1

Gradients and straight line graphs

Exercise 3

Find the gradient of the straight line joining A to B when

1 A is (0, 0) and B is (2, 2)

2 A is (2, 1) and B is (3, 3)

3 A is (0, 2) and B is (1, 1)

4 A is (1, 4) and B is (2, 1)

5 A garden path has a gradient of $\frac{1}{4}$. What is h?

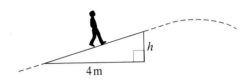

6 A ski slope has a gradient of $\frac{1}{2}$. What is h?

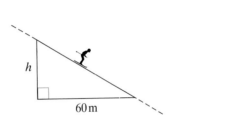

7 The gradient of a crane jib is 2. Find d.

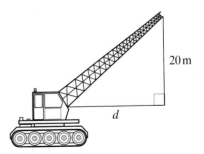

8 A tree leans with gradient 12. Find d.

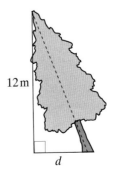

For Questions 9–12, write down the gradient and y intercept and then sketch the graph of the equation.

9 $y = x + 1$

10 $y = 2x - 1$

11 $y = \frac{1}{2}x + 4$

12 $y = 3x$

For Questions 13–16, write down the equations of the lines

13 with gradient 2, passing through $(0, 1)$

14 with gradient $\frac{1}{2}$, passing through $(0, 3)$

15 with gradient -1, passing through $(0, 2)$

16 with gradient $-\frac{1}{2}$, passing through $(0, -1)$

For Questions 17–20, write down the equations of the lines that are parallel to

17 $y = x + 3$ passing through $(0, 2)$

18 $y = \frac{1}{2}x - 7$ passing through $(0, 1)$

19 $y = -2x + 1$ passing through $(0, -1)$

20 $y = -\frac{1}{4}x + 5$ passing through $(0, -2)$

Find where the graph crosses the axes and sketch the graph for each of these.

21 $x + y = 5$

22 $x + 2y = 4$

23 $3x + y = 6$

24 $x - y = 3$

Exercise 3★

Find the gradient of the straight line joining A to B when

1 A is $(0, 0)$ and B is $(3, 1)$

2 A is $(1, -1)$ and B is $(2, 1)$

3 A is $(-1, 1)$ and B is $(1, 0)$

4 A is $(-1, 3)$ and B is $(1, 1)$

5 The gradient of a kite string is 6. Find h.

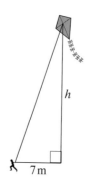

h

7 m

6 The leaning tower of Pisa leans with gradient 10. What is d?

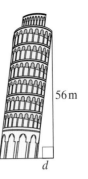

56 m

d

7 Part of the ride on a roller coaster has a gradient of -2. What is d?

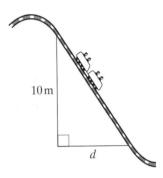

10 m

d

8 A shed roof has a gradient of $\frac{1}{3}$. Find w, the width of the shed.

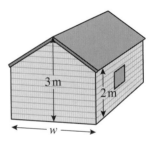

3 m

2 m

w

For Questions 9−12, write down the gradient and y intercept and then sketch the graph of the equation.

9 $y = 3x + 2$

10 $y = \frac{1}{4}x - 1$

11 $y = -2x$

12 $y = 2 - x$

For Questions 13−16, write down the equations of the lines

13 with gradient 3, passing through $(0, -1)$

14 with gradient $-\frac{1}{4}$, passing through $(0, 2)$

15 with gradient 1, passing through $(1, 1)$

16 with gradient 2, passing through $(3, 1)$

For Questions 17−20, write down the equations of the lines that are parallel to

17 $y = \frac{1}{3}x - 1$ passing through $(0, 4)$

18 $y = 4x + 8$ passing through $(0, -2)$

19 $y = -0.4x + 7$ passing through $(0, 1)$

20 $y = 0.2x + 3$ passing through $(0, 0)$

Find where the graph crosses the axes and sketch the graph for each of these.

21 $4x + y = 12$

22 $x + 3y = 15$

23 $x - 5y = 10$

24 $2x - 7y = 14$

Basic geometry, constructions and loci

Exercise 4

Use a compass and ruler to draw the following. Remember to show all your construction arcs.

1 An equilateral triangle of sides 7 cm.

2 A triangle of sides 7 cm, 8 cm and 9 cm.

3 The perpendicular bisector of the line AB where AB = 8 cm.

4 Angles of 30°, 60° and 45°.

5 In a party game, a valuable prize is hidden within a triangle formed by an Oak tree (O), an Apple tree (A) and a Plum tree (P).

   a Given that OA = 16 m, AP = 18 m and OP = 20 m construct the triangle OAP using a scale of 1 cm = 2 m.

   b The prize is equidistant from the Apple tree and the Plum tree and 12 m from the Oak tree. By careful construction find the distance of the prize from the Plum tree.

Calculate the size of each lettered angle.

6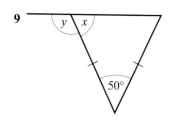

7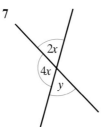

8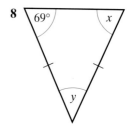

9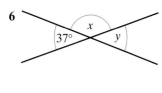

10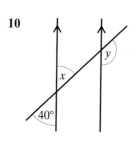

11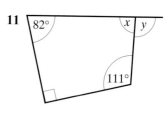

12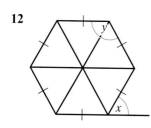

13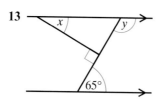

14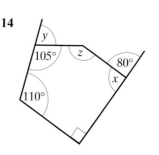

Exercise 4★

1 A regular decagon has ten sides. Calculate
   a the size of the exterior angles.
   b the size of the interior angles.
   c the sum of the interior angles.

2 The angle sum of a regular polygon is 3600°. Calculate
   a the number of sides of this polygon.
   b the exterior angle of this polygon.

3 The rectangle ABCD represents a map of an area
   30 m × 60 m. A mobile phone mast, M, is to be placed such
   that it is equidistant from A and B and 20 m from point E,
   such that BE : EC = 1 : 2.
   a Draw the map using a scale drawing of 1 cm = 5 m.
   b Showing your construction lines clearly, find the
      shortest distance of M from D.

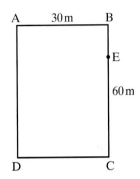

Calculate the size of each lettered angle.

4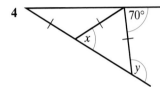

5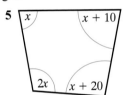

6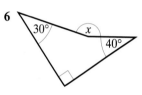

7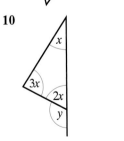

8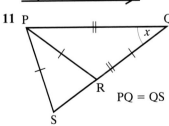

9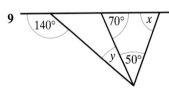

10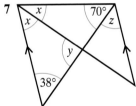

11 P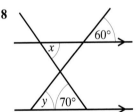
PQ = QS

12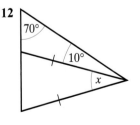

13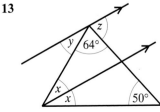

14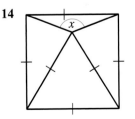

15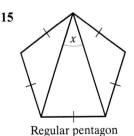
Regular pentagon

Sets 1

Basic principles and Venn diagrams

Exercise 5

1 Write down two more members of each of these sets.

    a {3, 6, 9, 12, ...}

    c {football, cricket, swimming,...}

    b {−1, −2, −3, ...}

    d {Ford, Toyota, Rolls-Royce, ...}

2 Describe the sets in Question 1 by a rule.

3 List these sets.

    a {even numbers between 1 and 9}

    c {months of the year beginning with J}

    b {square numbers between 2 and 20}

    d {colours on traffic lights}

4 Which of these statements are true and which are false?

    a $3 \in$ {odd numbers}

    c dog $\notin$ {animals with four legs}

    b $5 \notin$ {factors of 10}

    d triangle $\in$ {polygons}

5 Which of these are examples of the empty set?

    a {square numbers between 10 and 15}

    c {fish with teeth}

    b {birds with four legs}

    d {common factors of 32 and 45}

6 ξ = {positive integers less than 11}

    A = {multiples of 2}   B = {multiples of 4}

    a Illustrate this information on a Venn diagram.

    b List the set A′ and describe it in words.

    c What is $n(\text{B}')$?

    d Is B $\subset$ A? Explain your answer.

7 Draw Venn diagrams to illustrate these statements.

    a A ∩ B = ∅

    c A ∩ B = A

    b A ∩ B ≠ ∅

    d A ∪ B = A

8 ξ = { A, E, I, O, U }, W = {capital letters that have straight lines in them},
S = {capital letters that have curved parts in them}

    a List the sets W, W′, S and S′.

    b Draw a Venn diagram to represent the information.

    c What is **i** W ∪ S   **ii** W ∩ S?

9 ξ = {Suzy's clothes}, D = {Dresses}, R = {Red clothes} and G = {Green clothes}

    a D ∩ R = ∅. Describe what this means in words.

    b D ⊂ G. Describe what this means in words.

    c Illustrate all this information on a Venn diagram.

10 The following information was obtained about all the fast food restaurants in a town.

Six sold beefburgers and pizzas, four sold pizzas only, nine sold beefburgers, while two served neither beefburgers nor pizzas.

   a Draw a Venn diagram to represent all of this information

   b How many fast food restaurants are there in the town?

Exercise 5★

1 Write down two more members of these sets.

   a {4, 8, 12, 16, …}   **b** {10, 100, 1000, …}

   c {dog, cat, rabbit, …}   **d** {oak, ash, pine, …}

2 Describe the sets in Question 1 by a rule.

3 List these sets.

   a {all prime factors of 24}   **b** {all factors of 24}

   c {colours of the rainbow}   **d** {seasons of the year}

4 Which of these statements are true and which are false?

   a circle ∈ {polygons}   **b** $y = x + 2 \notin$ {straight line graphs with gradient 2}

   c $-1 \notin$ {solutions of $x^2 = 1$}   **d** square $\notin$ {parallelograms}

5 A Venn diagram consists of three sets A, B and C, such that $A \cap B \neq \varnothing$, $A \cap C = \varnothing$ and $C \subset B$. Draw a Venn diagram to show this information.

6 ξ = {odd number less than 21}, M = {multiples of 5}, F = {factors of 20}

   a Why is $10 \in M$ false?   **b** List M.

   c List F.   **d** List M ∩ F.

7 ξ = {even numbers less than 15}, A = {multiples of 4}
B satisfies $A \cap B = \varnothing$ and $n(B) = 4$.
What is $A \cup B$?

8 $n(\xi) = 17$, $n(B') = 9$ and $n(A' \cap B) = 6$

   a Find $n(B)$

   b Find $n(A \cap B)$

   c Draw a Venn diagram to illustrate this information.

9 A class of 30 students was asked to choose **at least** one option subject from list A and list B. Two students forgot to hand their forms in. Of the rest, twenty two chose list A and twenty five chose list B.

   a Draw a Venn diagram to illustrate this information.

   b How many students chose both options?

10 There are 30 Widgets, and every Widget is a Woodle.
There are 20 Wopets, half of which are Woodles. No Wopet is a Widget.
Half of all Woodles are Widgets.

   a Draw a Venn diagram to represent this information.

   b How many Woodles are neither Widgets nor Wopets?

1 a Write the number 385 000 in standard form.

  b Write the number 3.25×10^3 as an ordinary number.

2 a Write the number 36.5782 correct to 2 decimal places.

  b Write the number 36.5782 correct to 2 significant figures.

3 a Calculate $(4.8 \times 10^5) \div (1.2 \times 10^3)$, giving your answer in standard form to 3 significant figures.

  b Calculate $(4.8 \times 10^5) + (1.2 \times 10^3)$, giving your answer in standard form to 3 significant figures.

4 a Calculate $(3 \times 10^3) \times (4 \times 10^2)$, giving your answer in standard form to 3 significant figures.

  b Calculate $(3 \times 10^3) - (4 \times 10^2)$, giving your answer in standard form to 3 significant figures.

5 a Find 30% of £15.40.

  b Decrease £48.60 by 12%.

6 a Simplify the expression $3ba + 4ab - ba + 2ab$.

  b Simplify the expression $4xy - x(y - 3)$.

  c Simplify the expression $3ab \times a^2$.

7 a Solve the equation $2(3x + 1) = 20$.

  b Solve the equation $2(4a - 3) - (2a + 5) = 10$.

  c Solve the equation $7 - 2x = 3x - 8$.

8 Three consecutive numbers sum to 525.

  a If the first of the consecutive numbers is x, what is the second number?

  b Write down an equation in x.

  c Solve your equation to find x.

9 Which two of the following lines are parallel?

  $x - 3y = 12, \quad 3y + x = 5, \quad y = 3x - 2, \quad 6y - 2x = 7$

10 Find the gradient of the line through these pairs of points.

  a P = (1, 5) and Q = (3, 9)   **b** C = (4, 4) and D = (1, 16)

11 a A road has a gradient of $\frac{1}{20}$. What is the value of d?

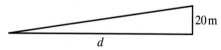

                                         20 m

                              d

  b The line joining A = (2, 5) to B = (6, q) has a gradient of $\frac{1}{2}$. Find the value of q.

12 a Construct triangle ABC, with AB = 7 cm, angle BAC = 75° and angle ABC = 60°.

  b Measure AC.

13 a Construct triangle PQR such that PQ = 8 cm, $\angle$PQR = 50°, and $\angle$RPQ = 80°.

  b Construct the perpendicular from R to intersect PQ at S.

  c Measure RS, and hence calculate the area of $\triangle$PQR.

14 In the diagram, ABC and AED are straight lines.
BE and CD are parallel. Angle BAE = 32° and angle EDC = 68°.
Work out the value of p.

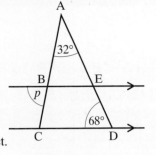

15 a Draw axes on graph paper with $-8 \leqslant x \leqslant 8$ and $-8 \leqslant y \leqslant 8$.
  b Draw the graph of the line $y = 3x + 2$.
  c Draw the graph of the line $x + 2y = 8$.
  d Write down the coordinates of the point where the two lines intersect.

16 Write down the gradient, intercept and
equation of the lines shown on the diagram.

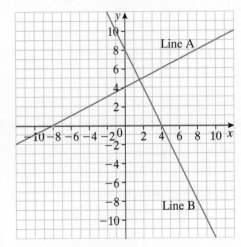

17 The Venn diagram shows four events
A, B, C, and D.

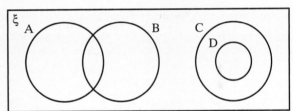

A ⊂ B	C ∪ D = D
A ∩ B ≠ ∅	A ∪ C = ξ
C ∪ D = C	A ∩ C = ∅

Choose a statement from the box that correctly describes the relationship between
  a A and C
  b D and C
  c A and B

18 $n(\xi) = 20$, $n(B') = 7$, $n(A' \cap B) = 6$
  a Find $n(B)$.
  b Find $n(A \cap B)$.

19 ξ = {all triangles}, A = {isosceles triangles}, B = {right angled triangles}
  a Draw a Venn diagram to illustrate the sets A and B.
  b Calculate the three angles of a member of A ∩ B
  C = {equilateral triangles}
  c Add set C to your Venn diagram.

20 ξ = {positive whole numbers less than 19}, A = {multiples of 2}, B = {multiples of 3}
  a List the set A ∩ B.
  b Describe the set A ∩ B.
  c Describe the set A'.
  d List the set A' ∩ B.
  e Describe the set A' ∩ B.

Number 2

Indices, standard form (negative indices), ratio, fractions and proportion

Exercise 6

Write these as a single power and then calculate the answer.

1 $2^2 \times 2^3$ **2** $3^2 \times 3^4$ **3** $4^2 \times 4^4$ **4** $5^3 \times 5^4$

5 $10^3 \times 10^6$ **6** $2^7 \div 2^3$ **7** $3^{11} \div 3^8$ **8** $4^{15} \div 4^{12}$

9 $5^{50} \div 5^{47}$ **10** $10^{100} \div 10^{94}$ **11** $(2^2)^3$ **12** $(3^2)^3$

13 $(4^4)^2$ **14** $(5^2)^4$ **15** $(10^3)^4$

Calculate the following showing all of your working.

16 $\frac{3}{7} + \frac{2}{5}$ **17** $\frac{3}{7} - \frac{2}{5}$ **18** $\frac{3}{7} \times \frac{2}{5}$ **19** $\frac{3}{7} \div \frac{2}{5}$

20 $2\frac{3}{5} + 1\frac{1}{7}$ **21** $2\frac{3}{5} - 1\frac{1}{7}$ **22** $2\frac{3}{5} \times 1\frac{1}{7}$ **23** $2\frac{3}{5} \div 1\frac{1}{7}$

24 Divide 36 m in the ratio of 1 : 2.   **25** Divide 105 kg in the ratio of 3 : 4.

26 Divide $400 in the ratio of 2 : 3.   **27** Divide 360 minutes in the ratio of 4 : 5.

28 Divide £133 in the ratio of 1 : 2 : 4.   **29** Divide 352 km in the ratio of 2 : 3 : 6.

Write the following in standard form correct to 3 significant figures.

30 0.012 345   **31** 0.012 355   **32** 0.000 159 5   **33** 0.008 888

34 $(1.25 \times 10^{-2}) \times (3.45 \times 10^5)$ **35** $(7.58 \times 10^{-5}) \times (1.35 \times 10^{12})$

36 $(7.25 \times 10^{-3}) \times (3.45 \times 10^{-10})$ **37** $(8.5 \times 10^{-2}) \times (3.45 \times 10^{-7})$

38 $(1.25 \times 10^{-2}) \div (3.45 \times 10^5)$ **39** $(7.58 \times 10^{-5}) \div (1.35 \times 10^{12})$

40 $(7.25 \times 10^{-3}) \div (3.45 \times 10^{-10})$ **41** $(8.5 \times 10^{-2}) \div (3.45 \times 10^{-7})$

42 Four tonnes of limestone blocks cost $600. Find the cost of

     a 1 tonne   **b** 11 tonnes   **c** 500 kg.

43 Seven identical pens cost €8.40. Find the cost of

     a one pen   **b** five pens.   **c** a dozen pens.

44 Stella Pajunas typed 216 words in 1 minute in Chicago, U.S.A. to set a new world record. If she maintained this rate, how many words would you expect her to type in

     a 45 seconds   **b** 50 seconds   **c** an hour?

45 Avind Pandya of India ran backwards from Los Angeles to New York, U.S.A. in 107 days covering 5000 km.

     a If he maintained this rate, how far would you expect him to travel in

         i 1 day   **ii** a year?

     b How long would it have taken him to travel

         i 10 km   **ii** 3500 m?

     c Calculate his speed in mm/sec writing your answer in standard form to 3 significant figures.

Exercise 6★

Write these as a single power and then calculate the answer.

1 $7^5 \times 7^7 \div 7^9$ **2** $8^{11} \times 8^9 \div 8^{15}$ **3** $(5^3)^2 \div 5^4$ **4** $(11^5)^2 \div 11^8$

5 $8^5 \div 64$ **6** $14\,641 \div 11^2$ **7** $1024 \div 8^2$ **8** $36^5 \div 6^2$

9 $125^3 \div 25^2$ **10** $\dfrac{128^2}{4 \times 16^3}$

Calculate the following, showing all of your working.

11 $\dfrac{2}{5} \times \dfrac{5}{11} \times \dfrac{3}{8}$ **12** $\dfrac{1}{3} + \dfrac{4}{7} - \dfrac{2}{15}$ **13** $\dfrac{4}{5} \div \dfrac{2}{7} \times \dfrac{3}{14}$ **14** $\dfrac{1}{7} \div \left(\dfrac{3}{5}\right)^2$

15 $1 \times 1\frac{1}{2} \times 1\frac{1}{3} \times 1\frac{1}{4} \times 1\frac{1}{5} \times 1\frac{1}{6} \times 1\frac{1}{7}$ **16** $\left(2\frac{3}{7}\right)^2 \div \left(1\frac{3}{7}\right)^2$

17 The ratio of $5 : x$ is equal to the ratio of $x : 20$. Calculate the value of x.

18 A bed of roses consists of m roses. The ratio of pink roses to white roses is $2 : 3$.
Find the number of pink roses expressed in terms of m.

19 Xavier, Yi and Zazoo decide to share their lottery winnings of £11 000 such that Yi has three times as much as Zazoo and Xavier has a half of Yi's winnings.
How much should each receive?

20 The plan for an office block is produced to a scale of $1 : 50$.
    a Find the length, in mm, which represents the height of the building on the plan if the actual height is 25 m.
    b Find the area of the actual front door, in m², if the door on the plan has an area of 80 cm².

Write the following in standard form correct to 3 significant figures:

21 $(1.36 \times 10^{-3})^2$ **22** $(3.75 \times 10^{-5})^2 \times (4.35 \times 10^{-7})^2$

23 $\sqrt{5.785 \times 10^{-12}}$ **24** $\sqrt{\dfrac{3.85 \times 10^{-9}}{1.47 \times 10^{-3}}}$

25 If $p = 9.47 \times 10^{-5}$ and $q = 4.31 \times 10^{-3}$, find the following in standard form correct to 3 significant figures.
    a pq **b** pq^2 **c** p^2q **d** $\left(\dfrac{p}{q}\right)^2$

26 The smallest mammal is the Kitti's hog-nosed bat in Thailand which has a body length of 29 mm.
Find this length in km in standard form correct to 3 significant figures.

27 The biggest known star is the M-class supergiant Betelgeuse which has a diameter of 980 million km.
    a Assuming it to be a sphere, calculate its surface area in mm², giving your answer in standard form correct to 3 significant figures.
    b Given that the Earth has a radius of 6370 km, express its surface area as a percentage of Betelgeuse's. Give your answer in standard form correct to 3 significant fgures.
    (The surface area of a sphere $= 4\pi r^2$, where r is the radius of the sphere.)

28 Kaylan Ramji Sain of India grew a moustache to a length of 339 mm from 1976 until 1993.
Calculate the speed of his moustache growth in km/s . Give your answer in standard form correct to 3 significant figures.

Algebra 2

Simplifying fractions, indices, equations, formulae and inequalities

Exercise 7

Simplify these:

1 $\frac{2x}{2}$ **2** $\frac{4z}{2}$ **3** $\frac{5y}{y}$

4 $\frac{10x}{5x}$ **5** $\frac{2xy}{4y}$ **6** $\frac{9x^2}{3x}$

7 $\frac{8y}{4y^2}$ **8** $\frac{a^2b}{ab}$ **9** $\frac{2}{3} \times \frac{x}{2}$

10 $\frac{3}{x} \times \frac{x}{4}$ **11** $\frac{a}{5} \times \frac{10}{a}$ **12** $\frac{x^2 \times y^2}{y \times x}$

13 $\frac{3}{4} \div \frac{3}{4x}$ **14** $\frac{x}{4} \div \frac{x}{8}$ **15** $\frac{4}{x^2} \div \frac{2}{x}$

16 $\frac{y}{x} \div \frac{y}{x}$ **17** $\frac{x}{2} + \frac{x}{4}$ **18** $\frac{x}{2} + \frac{x}{3}$

19 $\frac{x}{2} + \frac{3x}{4}$ **20** $\frac{x}{5} + \frac{2x}{3}$ **21** $\frac{x}{2} - \frac{x}{4}$

22 $\frac{x}{3} - \frac{x}{6}$ **23** $\frac{3x}{4} - \frac{x}{3}$ **24** $\frac{x}{2} - \frac{y}{2}$

Solve these equations.

25 $x^2 = 1$ **26** $x^2 + 1 = 10$ **27** $2x^2 = 50$

28 $2x^2 - 1 = 31$ **29** $\sqrt{x} = 4$ **30** $\sqrt{x} + 1 = 2$

31 $\sqrt{x + 1} = 2$ **32** $2\sqrt{x} + 1 = 5$

For Questions 33–36 you will need the following formulae.

Area of a triangle $= \frac{1}{2} \times$ base $\times$ height   Circumference of a circle $= 2\pi r$

Area of a parallelogram $=$ base $\times$ perpendicular height   Area of a circle $= \pi r^2$

33 The base of a triangle is 3 cm and its area is $6\,\text{cm}^2$. Find its height.

34 The circumference of a circle is 22 cm. Find its radius.

35 The base of a parallelogram is 12 cm and its area is $60\,\text{cm}^2$. Find its perpendicular height.

36 The area of a circle is $76\,\text{cm}^2$. Find its radius.

Use the rules of indices to simplify these, giving your answer in index form.

37 a $2^3 \times 2^5$ **b** $a^2 \times a^4$ **38 a** $2^2 \times 2^4 \times 2^6$ **b** $a^2 \times a^3 \times a^4$

39 a $3^8 \div 3^4$ **b** $a^7 \div a^3$ **40 a** $(2^4)^2$ **b** $(a^4)^3$

Solve the following inequalities and show the results on a number line.

41 $x + 1 < 2$ **42** $x - 1 \leqslant 3$ **43** $2x + 3 \geqslant 5$ **44** $3x - 1 < 8$

Exercise 7★

Simplify these.

1 $\dfrac{3x}{9}$ **2** $\dfrac{12}{3x}$ **3** $\dfrac{16z}{8z}$

4 $\dfrac{4a^2}{2a}$ **5** $\dfrac{12xy^2}{4xy}$ **6** $\dfrac{4x^2y}{2xy^2}$

7 $\dfrac{a^2bc^3}{ac^2}$ **8** $\dfrac{16x^3y}{4xy}$ **9** $\dfrac{3x}{2} \times \dfrac{x}{9}$

10 $\dfrac{2x}{3} \times \dfrac{6}{x}$ **11** $\dfrac{4a^2 \times 3}{3 \times 8a}$ **12** $\dfrac{x}{y} \times \dfrac{z}{y} \times \dfrac{y^2}{x}$

13 $\dfrac{5}{3x} \div \dfrac{10}{x}$ **14** $\dfrac{3x}{4} \div \dfrac{3x}{4}$ **15** $\dfrac{x^2}{y^2} \div \dfrac{5z}{y^2}$

16 $\dfrac{4ab^2}{c} \div \dfrac{ab}{c^2}$ **17** $\dfrac{x}{3} + \dfrac{3x}{4}$ **18** $\dfrac{2x}{3} + \dfrac{3x}{5}$

19 $\dfrac{1}{x} + \dfrac{2}{x}$ **20** $\dfrac{1}{2x} + \dfrac{2}{3x}$ **21** $\dfrac{3a}{10} - \dfrac{a}{5}$

22 $\dfrac{4z}{3} - \dfrac{2z}{5}$ **23** $\dfrac{3x}{2} - \dfrac{1}{2}$ **24** $\dfrac{1}{x} - \dfrac{2}{5x}$

Solve these equations.

25 $x^2 - 5 = 20$ **26** $3x^2 + 1 = 49$ **27** $\dfrac{x^2}{2} + 3 = 11$

28 $\dfrac{x^2 + 3}{2} = 6$ **29** $\sqrt{x} + 8 = 10$ **30** $3\sqrt{x} - 2 = 7$

31 $2\sqrt{x} + 5 = 1$ **32** $\dfrac{3\sqrt{x + 1}}{5} = 6$

For Questions 33–36 you will need the following formulae.

Area of a triangle $= \frac{1}{2} \times$ base $\times$ height   Circumference of a circle $= 2\pi r$

Speed $=$ Distance $\div$ time   Area of a circle $= \pi r^2$

33 The base of a triangle is 7.3 cm and its area is 21.7 cm². Find its height.

34 The circumference of a circle is 36 cm. Find its radius and area.

35 A car is travelling at 21 m/s. How long does it take to travel 106 m?

36 The area of a circle is 18 cm². Find its radius and circumference.

Use the rules of indices to simplify these, giving your answer in index form.

37 a $3 \times 3^5 \times 3^4$ **b** $a \times a^3 \times a^2$ **38 a** $5^9 \div 5^2$ **b** $x^{12} \div x^{10}$

39 a $(4^3)^2$ **b** $(y^6)^3$ **40 a** $(7^3)^4 \div 7^8$ **b** $(z^2)^4 \div z^5$

Solve the following inequalities and show the results on a number line.

41 $5x - 1 \leqslant 9$ **42** $3x - 1 > x + 7$ **43** $4(1 - x) > 12$ **44** $2 + x \geqslant 2(x + 2)$

Graphs 2

Simultaneous equations and inequalities

Exercise 8

1 Copy and complete these tables, and then draw both graphs on one set of axes.

x	0	2	4
$y = x + 1$			

x	0	2	4
$y = 5 - x$			

Solve the simultaneous equations $y = x + 1$ and $y = 5 - x$ using your graphs.

2 Copy and complete these tables, and then draw both graphs on one set of axes.

x	0	2	4
$y = 3 - x$			

x	0	2	4
$y = x - 1$			

Solve the simultaneous equations $y = 3 - x$ and $y = x - 1$ using your graphs.

Solve the following simultaneous equations graphically, using $0 \leqslant x \leqslant 6$ in each question.

3 $y = \frac{1}{2}x + 2, y = x$

4 $y = 2x - 1, y = \frac{1}{2}x$

5 $y = \frac{1}{2}x + 1, y = 4 - x$

6 $y = 1 - \frac{1}{2}x, y = 2x - 2$

For questions 7–12 describe the **unshaded** region in each graph.

7
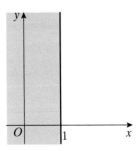

8
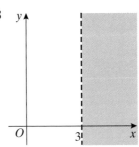

9
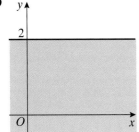

10
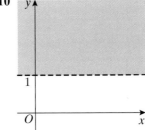

11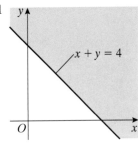

12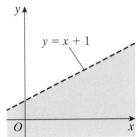

Illustrate each inequality on a graph, shading the unwanted region.

13 $x > 2$ **14** $y \leqslant 5$ **15** $x \leqslant 4$ **16** $y \geqslant 3$

Describe the **unshaded** region in each graph.

17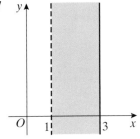

18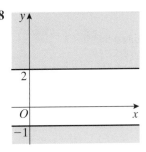

Illustrate each inequality on a graph, shading the unwanted region.

19 $y < 1$ or $y > 2$ **20** $3 \leqslant x \leqslant 6$

Exercise 8★

1 On one set of axes, draw the graphs of $y = x + 3$ and $x + y = 6$ for $0 \leqslant x \leqslant 6$.
Then solve the simultaneous equations $y = x + 3$ and $x + y = 6$ using your graphs.

2 On one set of axes, draw the graphs of $y = 3 - x$ and $y = 2x - 4$ for $0 \leqslant x \leqslant 6$.
Then solve the simultaneous equations $y = 3 - x$ and $y = 2x - 4$ using your graphs.

Solve the following simultaneous equations graphically, using $0 \leqslant x \leqslant 6$ in each question.

3 $y = 3x - 5$ and $y = x - 1$
4 $y = 4 - \frac{1}{2}x$ and $y = 6 - x$
5 $y = 6 - \frac{1}{2}x$ and $y = x - 2$
6 $y = \frac{1}{2}x - 2$ and $y = 6 - 2x$

For questions 7-12 describe the **unshaded** region in each graph.

7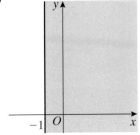

8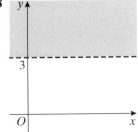

9

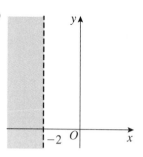

10

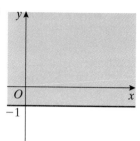

11

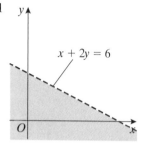

$x + 2y = 6$

12

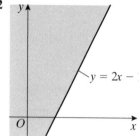

$y = 2x - 1$

Illustrate each inequality on a graph, shading the unwanted region.

13 $x < -2$ **14** $y \geqslant -4$

15 $x + y \leqslant 8$ **16** $2x + y \geqslant 4$

Describe the **unshaded** region in each graph.

17

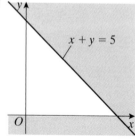

$x + y = 5$

18

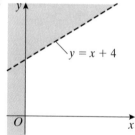

$y = x + 4$

Illustrate each inequality on a graph, shading the unwanted region.

19 $x + y \geqslant 2$ and $x < 2$ **20** $y \leqslant x + 1$ and $y > -1$

Shape and space 2

Tangent ratio

Exercise 9

For Questions 1–6, find the value of side x.

1
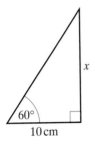

2
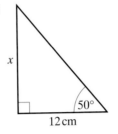

3
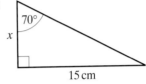

4
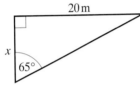

5
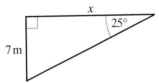

6
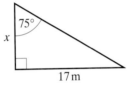

For Questions 7–12, find the value of angle θ.

7
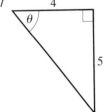

8
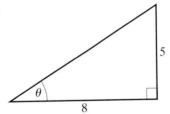

9
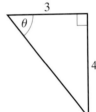

10
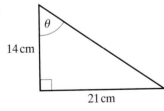

11
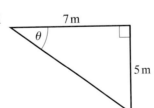

12
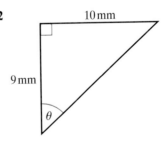

13 A bird watcher spots an eagle perched at the top of a tree of height h metres. The angle of elevation from the ornithologist to the eagle is 20° and she stands 100 m from the base of the tree. Find h.

14 A telephone engineer stands at the top of a telegraph pole of height 15 m. He spots his toolbox which is *x* metres from the base of the pole at an angle of depression of 35°.
Find *x*.

15 Lighthouse A is 30 km due South of lighthouse B. Port C is 60 km due West of A.
Calculate the bearing of

    a C from B   **b** B from C.

16 Find the area of an equilateral triangle with total perimeter 60 cm.

Exercise 9★

For Questions 1–4, find the lengths of sides *x* and *y*.

1

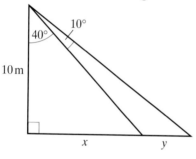

2

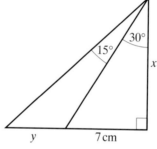

3

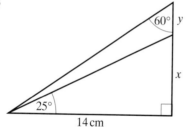

4

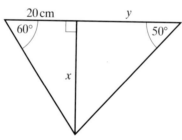

For Questions 5–8, find the value of angle θ.

5

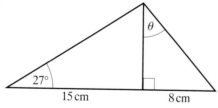

6

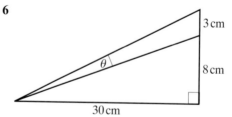

7

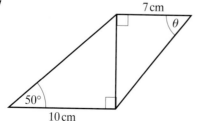

8

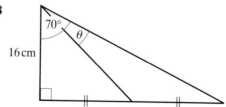

9 Rob skis down a straight slope from point A to point B. The difference in height between these two points is 125 m, and the actual distance AB as viewed on a map is 375 m. Calculate the angle of this ski slope.

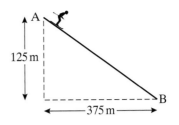

10 Find the angle that the line $y = 3x - 7$ makes with the x-axis.

11 Find the angle that the line $2x + 3y - 4 = 0$ makes with the y-axis.

12 An area of an equilateral triangle is 1000 cm². Calculate the perimeter of the triangle.

13 An equilateral triangle has sides of 10 m. Its area is equal to that of a circle. Calculate the circumference of the circle.

14 From the top of a cliff of height y m the angle of depression of a Channel swimmer at X is 30°. She swims directly towards the base of the cliff such that, 1 minute later, at Y, the angle of depression from the top of the cliff to the swimmer is 50°. Given that her speed between X and Y is 0.75 m/s, find the height of the cliff.

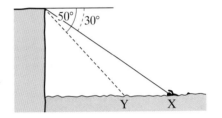

Handling data 2

Data collection and display, frequency tables and averages

Exercise 10

1 These are the maximum temperatures in °C that a gardener recorded one week.

21, 20, 23, 20, 22, 20, 21

Find the mean, median and mode of these temperatures.

2 In a primary school competition to grow the tallest sunflower, the following heights (in metres) were obtained.

1.32, 1.87, 2.03, 1.56, 1.95, 1.48, 1.12, 2.15

a Calculate the mean and median heights of these sunflowers.

b The 2.15 m height had been recorded incorrectly and was actually 2.75 m. Calculate the new mean height.

3 The day after a school disco a sample of pupils were asked to give it a rating from A to E, A being excellent and E being dreadful. The following results were obtained.

D, B, E, E, C, A, E, B, A, B, E, A, B, D, A, D, D, A, D, B, A, D, E, C, E, A, E, E, A, A

a Construct a tally chart and then draw a bar chart to display this information.

b Can you draw any conclusions about the disco?

4 The following ingredients are needed to make a strawberry smoothie.

250 g of strawberries, 150 g of banana, 200 g yoghurt and 120 g of iced water.

Display this information in a pie chart, marking the size of the angles clearly.

5 Tara suspects that a die is biased. She throws it 50 times with the following results.

6 1 4 4 2 5 4 1 2 3 4 3 2 4 1 2 6 3 2 6 6 6 6 1 4
5 6 4 6 4 2 6 3 1 2 2 6 5 4 3 1 6 6 2 5 5 2 1 4 5

a Construct a tally chart for the data.

b Construct a bar chart to represent this information.

c Comment on Tara's suspicions.

6 These are the times, t, in seconds, that it took a group of students to solve a puzzle.

42, 67, 54, 79, 72, 56, 54, 47, 41, 41, 46, 42, 78, 71, 69, 70, 49, 62, 48, 78, 65, 42, 40, 51, 73,
77, 41, 65, 78, 73, 50, 67, 66, 44, 67, 50, 59, 55, 50, 51, 66, 41, 45, 69, 52, 58, 42, 44, 43, 68

a Construct a tally chart using the groups $40 \leqslant t < 45$, $45 \leqslant t < 50$ and so on.

b Draw a bar chart to represent this information.

c What percentage of the class took less than 1 minute to solve the puzzle?

7 This frequency table shows the times taken by competitors on a charity fun run.

Time (mins)	$60 \leqslant t < 70$	$70 \leqslant t < 80$	$80 \leqslant t < 90$	$90 \leqslant t < 100$	$100 \leqslant t < 110$	$110 \leqslant t < 120$
Frequency	8	14	26	17	13	7

   a How many competitors were there?

   b Draw a frequency polygon to display this information.

   c What percentage of the competitors took at least 100 minutes?

8 A group of ten girls has a mean height of 1.42 m.

   a What is the total height of all ten girls?
      One girl with height 1.57 m leaves the group.

   b What is the mean height of the remaining girls?

9 These are the number of goals Mark scored each match **last** season. 0, 1, 0, 0, 2, 0, 1, 1, 3, 0

   a Find the mean, median and mode of this data.

   b This season Mark has played in 12 games. The mean number of goals he has scored is 1. What is the mean number of goals he has scored over both seasons?

Exercise 10★

1 These are the results when a research group were asked to name their lucky number.
5, 7, 9, 1, 7, 3, 6, 7, 2, 4, 7, 0
Find the mean, median and mode of these numbers.

2 The lengths of tracks in minutes on a CD were as follows: 6.2, 3.6, 10.8, 2.4, 2.3, 8.7, 14.7, 10.9

   a Calculate the mean and median length of tracks on the CD.

   b The time of 10.9 had been misread and was actually 16.9. Calculate the correct mean.

3 These are the number of times that each pupil in 7R has been late this term.

   0, 4, 5, 1, 3, 4, 6, 0, 1, 2, 3, 0, 0, 2, 6, 5, 4, 0, 1, 3, 2, 0, 4, 3, 2, 1, 1, 4, 6, 0

   a Find the mean, median and mode of this data.

   b Which average would the head teacher prefer to use in his report to the Governors?

   c Draw a bar chart to display the information.

4 The pie chart shows the results of a school mock election
If Labour received 183 votes, how many pupils
voted altogether?

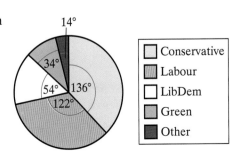

5 The weight marked on a cereal packet is 500 g. These are the weights in grams of fifty packets of cereal.

506, 507, 513, 502, 504, 507, 509, 505, 506, 515, 503, 508, 510, 500, 511, 505, 493, 514, 499, 501, 510, 506, 503, 516, 495, 519, 503, 507, 523, 508, 511, 517, 506, 497, 513, 516, 512, 503, 511, 504, 512, 501, 508, 505, 506, 509, 507, 513, 508, 521

  a Construct a tally chart using groups $490 \leqslant w < 495$, $495 \leqslant w < 500$ and so on up to $520 \leqslant w < 525$.

  b Draw a bar chart to display the information.

  c Does the evidence suggest that 500 g is a mean weight or a minimum weight?

6 This frequency table shows the speeds of some cars on a road.

Speed s km/h	$30 \leqslant s < 35$	$35 \leqslant s < 40$	$40 \leqslant s < 45$	$45 \leqslant s < 50$	$50 \leqslant s < 55$	$55 \leqslant s < 60$
Frequency	4	18	43	54	5	2

  a How many cars had their speeds recorded?

  b Draw a frequency polygon to display this information.

  c What do you think the speed limit is on this road? Give a reason for your answer.

7 This frequency table shows how much time per week 120 teenagers spent watching television.

Time t hrs	$0 \leqslant t < 2$	$2 \leqslant t < 4$	$4 \leqslant t < 6$	$6 \leqslant t < 8$	$8 \leqslant t < 10$	$10 \leqslant t < 12$	$12 \leqslant t \leqslant 14$
Frequency	18	12	10		21	25	19

  a What is the frequency for the group $6 \leqslant t < 8$?

  b Draw a bar chart to display the information.

  c What percentage watched between 4 and 10 hours of television per week?

8 A football team of eleven players has a mean height of 1.83 m. One player is injured and is replaced by a player of height 1.85 m. The new mean height of the team is now 1.84 m. What is the height of the injured player?

9 Sharon is doing a biology project using two groups of worms. The mean length of the first group of ten worms is 8.3 cm.

  a What is the total length of all the worms in the first group?

The mean of the second group of 8 worms is 10.7 cm.

  b Calculate the mean length of all eighteen worms.

Examination practice 2

1 Write each of these numbers as an ordinary number.
   a $(5 \times 10^{-2}) + (4 \times 10^{-4})$
   b $(5 \times 10^{-2}) \times (4 \times 10^{-4})$

2 Show that
   a $\frac{3}{5} \times \frac{15}{21} = \frac{3}{7}$
   b $3\frac{1}{4} + 2\frac{1}{3} = 5\frac{7}{12}$
   c $\frac{14}{15} \div \frac{7}{25} = 3\frac{1}{3}$

3 Share these amounts in the ratios given.
   a 767 kg in the ratio $5:8$
   b \$4.48 in the ratio $2:7:5$

4 £30 can be exchanged for 270 Egyptian pounds.
  How many Egyptian pounds would you get for £12?

5 A car travels for three hours, covering a distance of 147 miles.
  Work out its average speed in kilometres per hour, assuming 1 mile = 1.6 km.

6 A bullet from a machine gun travels at 108 m/s. Assuming that the bullet does not slow down, find the
  time, in seconds, that it takes to travel 3 km.

7 Simplify these.
   a $\dfrac{45a^5}{15a^3}$
   b $\dfrac{7x}{y} \div \dfrac{14x^2}{y}$
   c $\dfrac{8a^3}{3b} \times \dfrac{9b^2}{22a} \times \dfrac{11b}{4a^2}$

8 Write these as single fractions.
   a $\dfrac{a}{2} + \dfrac{b}{7}$
   b $\dfrac{3y}{5} - \dfrac{2y}{4}$
   c $\dfrac{7(x-3)}{4} + \dfrac{3(2-y)}{5}$

9 Solve these equations for x.
   a $2x^2 - 7 = 43$
   b $\dfrac{11 + \sqrt{x}}{3} = 5$
   c $\sqrt{\dfrac{3x^2 + 20}{2}} = 8$

10 The formula for converting a temperature, C, in degrees Celsius (°C) to a temperature, F, in degrees
   Fahrenheit (°F) is $\quad F = \dfrac{9C + 160}{5}$.
   a Use the formula to convert
      i 20°C to degrees Fahrenheit.
      ii 100°F to degrees Celsius.
   b What temperature is the same on both scales?

11 Simplify these.
   a $y^4 \times y^9$
   b $b^{16} \div b^7$
   c $8a^2 \times 2b^8$

12 Simplify these.
   a $b^2 \times b^4 \times b^3$
   b $(7a^4)^2$
   c $p^9 \div p$

13 Simplify these.
   a $\dfrac{21a^2bd}{48(ab)^2}$
   b $\dfrac{49a^5b^3c^7}{7a^3b^4c^4}$
   c $\dfrac{(3f)^2}{24f^5}(2f)^3$

14 Solve these inequalities and illustrate the answers on a number line.

   a $x - 8 > 4$ **b** $7x + 2 \leqslant 4x + 23$

15 n is an integer such that $-6 < n \leqslant 2$. List all the possible values of n.

16 a On graph paper draw x and y-axes such that $-2 \leqslant x \leqslant 12$ and $-2 \leqslant y \leqslant 12$.

   b On these axes draw both the lines $y = 2x - 1$ and $x + y = 11$.

   c Use your graph to solve the simultaneous equations $y = 2x - 1$ and $x + y = 11$.

   d Illustrate the region $y \geqslant 2x - 1$ and $x + y \leqslant 11$ by shading the **unwanted** regions.

17 Calculate the lengths x and y and the angle z in the diagrams below.

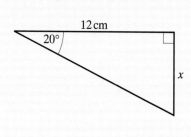 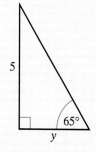 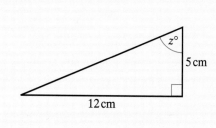

18 On a map of Derbyshire, Belper is 10 cm east of Ashbourne and Derby is 7 cm south of Belper. Draw a suitable diagram and **calculate** the bearing of Derby from Ashbourne.

19 The amounts of money, in pence, placed in the charity box over 20 days by a class of pupils is given in the table.

20	19	33	18	13	25	21	31	15	18
27	27	26	38	16	19	27	25	30	20

   a Find the mean, median and mode of these amounts.

The mean amount collected per day over the next 10 days was 22.2 pence.

   b Calculate the mean amount collected per day over the total period of 30 days.

20

Grade	Number of pupils
A	p
B	q
C	r
D	s
E	40

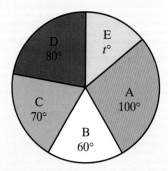

The table and the pie-chart show the number of grades that were obtained in a Russian examination by the pupils at Moscow Grammar School.

Find the values of p, q, r, s and t.

Number 3

Compound percentages, calculator work, HCF and LCM

Exercise 11

Copy and complete these tables:

1

% increase	multiply by
5	1.05
12	
25	
	1.75
	1.99

2

% decrease	multiply by
5	0.95
12	
25	
	0.25
	0.01

3 $500 is invested at 7% compound interest per year. Find the value of the investment after
  a 1 year
  b 2 years
  c 3 years
  d 4 years.

4 £100 is invested at 4% compound interest per year. Find the value of the investment after
  a 1 year
  b 2 years
  c 5 years
  d 10 years.

5 A valuable oil painting is worth €25 000 and appreciates by 5% per year.
  How much is it worth after
  a 1 year
  b 2 years
  c 5 years
  d 20 years?

6 A brand new car is purchased for £45 000 and depreciates by 8% per year.
  How much is it worth after
  a 1 year
  b 2 years
  c 5 years
  d 10 years?

7 Find the highest common factor of
  a 4 and 10
  b 5 and 30
  c 16 and 24
  d 14 and 30.

8 Find the lowest common multiple of
  a 3 and 4
  b 6 and 7
  c 15 and 40
  d 18 and 70.

Use your calculator to find the answer to the following, correct to 3 significant figures:

9 $1.2 + 1.2^2$

10 $1.2 + 1.2^2 + 1.2^3$

11 $\dfrac{251.7 + 3.6 \times 10^2}{2.5 \times 10^3}$

12 $4\frac{2}{7} + 1.35^3$

13 $\dfrac{11.2 + 3.7}{\sqrt{6.3}}$

14 $\dfrac{\sqrt{21.3}}{17.3 - 2.6}$

15 $\left(\dfrac{3.5 \times 10^3}{6.7 \times 10^2}\right)^2$

16 $\sqrt{5.75 \times 10^{12}}$

17 $(2^3 + 3^4 + 4^3 + 3^2)^2$

18 $\sqrt{3^4 + 3^4 + 3^4}$

19 $\sqrt{3.82 \times 10^7} \div \sqrt{6.7 \times 10^{-5}}$

20 $\sqrt{9.5^3 - 5.9^3}$

Exercise 11★

1 €2500 is invested at 6% compound interest. Calculate
  a its value after 5 years   **b** after how many years its value has doubled.

2 \$100 000 is invested at 3% compound interest. Calculate
  a its value after 10 years   **b** after how many years its value is increased by 50%.

3 An antique silk rug is worth £12 000 after it has appreciated by 5% for ten consecutive years. How much was it worth ten years ago?

4 A valuable wooden carving is valued at \$750 000 after it has appreciated by 12% for five consecutive years. How much was it worth
  a five years ago?   **b** two years ago?

5 A television is worth €525 after it has depreciated by 7% for three consecutive years. How much was it worth three years ago?

6 A farm tractor is worth £11 500 after it has depreciated by 9% for four consecutive years. How much was it worth
  a four years ago   **b** two years ago?

7 Find the HCF and LCM of
  a 60 and 70   **b** 140 and 84   **c** 42 and 70

8 Find the HCF and LCM of
  a $2x^2yz$ and $12xy^2z^2$ **b** $20pq$ and $35pq$ **c** $12a^2b^3c^4$ and $18a^4b^3c^2$

For Questions 9–14, use your calculator to find the answer correct to 3 significant figures.

9 $\left(\dfrac{1}{2.5 \times 10^{-3}} - \dfrac{1}{2.6 \times 10^{-3}}\right)^5$

10 $\sqrt{5 + \sqrt{5 + \sqrt{5 + \sqrt{5 + \sqrt{5}}}}}$

11 $\sqrt[3]{10 + \sqrt[3]{10 + \sqrt[3]{10 + \sqrt[3]{10 + \sqrt[3]{10}}}}}$

12 $\dfrac{1}{\sqrt{\pi^3 \times 10^{-3}}}$

13 $\sqrt[3]{5.5 \times 10^3 \times \tan(30)°}$

14 $\tan\left(\sqrt{\dfrac{10\pi^3}{\pi^2 - 1}}\right)°$

Algebra 3

Factorising, simplifying fractions, equations with fractions and simultaneous equations

Exercise 12

Factorise these completely.

1 $2a + 2b$

2 $3x - 6y$

3 $a^2 + 2a$

4 $5x - x^2$

5 $2x^2 - 4x$

6 $5a + 10a^2$

Simplify these.

7 $\dfrac{3x + 3y}{3}$

8 $\dfrac{2x + 4y}{2}$

9 $\dfrac{a + a^2}{a}$

10 $\dfrac{2a + 2b}{a + b}$

Solve for x.

11 $\dfrac{x}{2} = 5$

12 $\dfrac{2x}{3} = 4$

13 $\dfrac{x}{3} = \dfrac{1}{2}$

14 $\dfrac{2x}{5} = \dfrac{1}{10}$

15 $\dfrac{3x}{4} = 0$

16 $\dfrac{x}{4} + \dfrac{x}{2} = 1$

17 $\dfrac{2}{x} = 1$

18 $\dfrac{9}{x} = 3$

19 $\dfrac{5}{x} = -10$

20 $\dfrac{3}{x} = -\dfrac{1}{2}$

21 $\dfrac{2}{x} = \dfrac{3}{4}$

22 $\dfrac{16}{x} = x$

Solve these simultaneous equations by elimination.

23 $x + y = 3$ and $x - y = 1$

24 $2x + y = 7$ and $x - y = 2$

25 $x + y = 5$ and $x - 2y = 2$

26 $x + y = 5$ and $-x + y = 2$

27 $x + y = 4$ and $2x + y = 5$

28 $x + 3y = 4$ and $x + y = 2$

Solve these simultaneous equations by substitution.

29 $x = y$ and $x + 2y = 6$

30 $x = y - 2$ and $x + 4y = 3$

31 $y = x - 1$ and $5x + y = 11$

32 $x = y + 1$ and $2x + 3y = 7$

33 $y = 3x - 1$ and $y = 5x - 3$

34 $x = 2y + 1$ and $x = 4y - 1$

Solve these problems using simultaneous equations.

35 Find two numbers with a sum of 72 and a difference of 20.

36 Three apples and two bananas cost £1.90 while two apples and three bananas cost £2.10. Find the cost of an apple and the cost of a banana.

Exercise 12★

Factorise these completely.

1 $x^2 + 5x$

2 $7a - a^2$

3 $2x^2 + 6x$

4 $3x - 12x^2$

5 $a^2b + b^2a$

6 $4xy - 8x^2y^2$

Simplify these.

7 $\dfrac{3x + 6y}{3}$

8 $\dfrac{x^2 + 2x}{x}$

9 $\dfrac{ab + a^2b}{ab}$

10 $\dfrac{2x^2 + 2xy}{x + y}$

Solve for x.

11 $\dfrac{x}{8} = \dfrac{3}{4}$

12 $\dfrac{5x}{6} = \dfrac{1}{2}$

13 $\dfrac{x + 1}{4} = \dfrac{x - 2}{3}$

14 $\dfrac{(x - 4)}{5} = 0$

15 $\dfrac{3(x - 2)}{4} = 9$

16 $\dfrac{2x}{5} + x = 21$

17 $\dfrac{8}{x} = 4$

18 $\dfrac{3}{x} = 15$

19 $-\dfrac{1}{7} = \dfrac{7}{x}$

20 $\dfrac{9}{2x} = 6$

21 $\dfrac{2}{x} = \dfrac{x}{8}$

22 $x - \dfrac{64}{x} = 0$

Solve these simultaneous equations by elimination.

23 $2x + y = 9$ and $x - y = 3$

24 $3x + 2y = 13$ and $2x - y = 4$

25 $x + 3y = 7$ and $y - x = 1$

26 $x + y = 2$ and $2x + 3y = 5$

27 $3x + 2y = 8$ and $2x - 3y = 1$

28 $5x + 4y = 13$ and $2x + 3y = 8$

Solve these simultaneous equations by substitution.

29 $x = y - 3$ and $x + 2y = 9$

30 $y = x + 7$ and $3x + y = 11$

31 $y = x - 2$ and $4x - y = 11$

32 $x = y + 4$ and $2x + 5y = 22$

33 $y = 3x + 8$ and $x + 2y = 9$

34 $2x + 3y = 7$ and $x = 4y - 2$

Solve these problems using simultaneous equations.

35 Gemma is buying some trees for a conservation project. 20 ash trees and 30 beech trees will cost her $310 while 30 ash trees and 20 beech trees will cost her $290. Find the cost of each type of tree.

36 Rita finds that 10 minutes of phone calls and 20 text messages costs her £4, while 20 minutes of phone calls and thirty text messages costs her £7. Find the cost of a one minute phone call and the cost of one text message.

Graphs 3

Travel graphs

Exercise 13

1 Find the speed of the bicycle's journey shown in the distance–time graph.

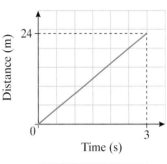

2 Find the speed of the boat's journey shown in the distance–time graph.

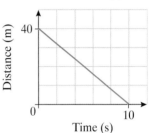

3 An insect's journey is shown in the distance–time graph. Find
   a the insect's outward journey speed in m/s
   b how long the insect remained stationary
   c the insect's return journey speed in m/s.

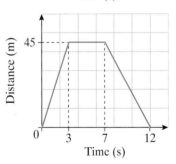

4 Luke leaves home at 08:00, and cycles to Martha's house at a speed of 20 km/h for one hour. He stays there for two hours before returning home at a speed of 30 km/h.
   a Draw a distance–time graph to illustrate Luke's journey.
   b Use this graph to find the time Luke returns home.

5 Find the acceleration of the boat's journey shown in the speed–time graph.

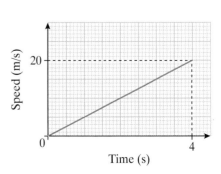

6 Find the acceleration of the train's journey shown in the speed–time graph.

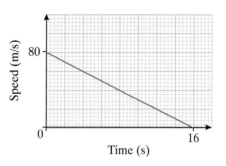

7 Johann's journey is shown in the speed–time graph. Find Johann's

   a initial acceleration

   b acceleration at 30 seconds

   c final acceleration

   d mean speed for the whole journey.

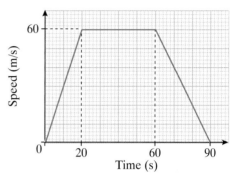

8 A model aeroplane accelerates from rest to 10 m/s in 20 s, remains at that speed for 30 s and then slows steadily to rest in 10 s.

   a Draw the speed–time graph for the aeroplane's journey.

   b Use this graph to find the aeroplane's

     i initial acceleration

     ii final acceleration

     iii mean speed over the whole 60 second journey.

Exercise 13★

1 Sketch distance–time graphs that show the journey of Michelle

   a going to school at a constant speed

   b returning from school at constant speed.

2 Sketch distance–time graphs that show the journey of Frank

   a going to the train station at a gradually increasing speed

   b returning from the train station at a gradually decreasing speed.

3 Sketch a distance–time graph for a flying duck such that its entire journey is described as:

   An initial constant speed, followed by a gradual reduction in speed until the duck is stationary, after which it gradually accelerates to reach a constant speed faster than its initial speed.

4 Mrs Lam leaves home for work at 07:00 driving at a constant speed of 60 km/h. After 45 minutes she increases her speed to 80 km/h for a further 45 minutes. She stays at work for 4 hours before she returns home at 70 km/h to meet Mr Lam who gets home at 2 pm.

   Draw a distance–time graph and use it to find out if Mrs Lam is late to meet her husband.

5 Sketch speed–time graphs that show

   a constant acceleration

   b zero acceleration.

   c constant deceleration.

6 Sketch speed–time graphs that show

   a increasing acceleration

   b constant speed

   c decreasing acceleration.

7 A hawk accelerates from rest to 12 m/s in 6 seconds followed by a further acceleration to 18 m/s in 3 seconds. It then remains at that speed for 10 seconds before retarding at x m/s^2 to rest.

   a Given that the hawk's total flight is 288 m, find x.

   b Draw the speed–time graph for the hawk's journey.

   c Use this graph to find the hawk's

     i initial acceleration.

     ii final acceleration.

     iii mean speed for the whole length of the hawk's flight.

8 In the school Sports Day, Ivan wins the 400 m in 62.5 seconds.

   a Calculate his average speed in

     i m/s   **ii** km/h.

   The speed–time graph of Ivan's race is shown.

   b Calculate his maximum speed in m/s.

   c Find his initial acceleration in m/s^2.

Shape and space 3

Sine and cosine ratios

Exercise 14

For Questions 1–6, find each side marked x.

1
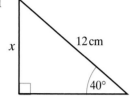

2
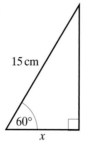

3
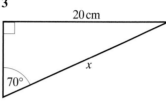

4
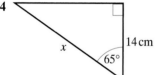

5
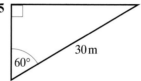

6
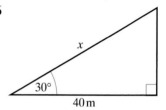

For Questions 7–12 , find the value of angle θ.

7
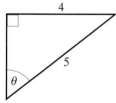

8
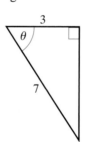

9
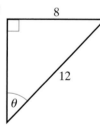

10
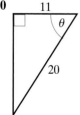

11
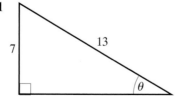

12
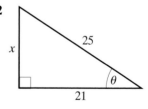

13 A 4.2 m ladder makes an angle of 20° with a vertical wall. Calculate the distance of the foot of the ladder from the base of the wall.

14 Jamila runs from point A on a constant bearing of 300° at 5m/s for 15 minutes at which point she stops at point B. Calculate how far Jamila has run

   a North from A.   **b** West from A.   **c** from A.

15 A straight wheelchair ramp is 12 m long and rises 225 cm. Find the angle the ramp makes with the horizontal.

16 An isosceles triangle has sides of 12 cm, 12 cm and 6 cm. Calculate

   a the internal angles

   b the area of the triangle.

Exercise 14★

For Questions 1–4, find the lengths of x and y.

1
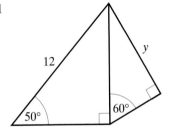

2
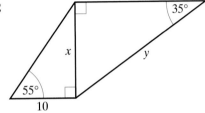

3
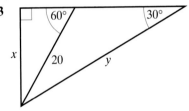

4
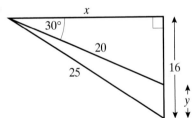

For Questions 5–8, find the value of θ.

5
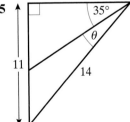

6
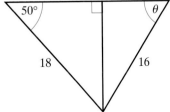

7
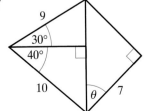

8
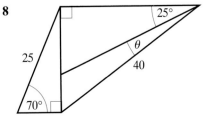

9 Raphael hikes from village A for 7 km on a bearing of 040° to village B. He then hikes 12 km on a bearing of 130° to village C. He needs to return back to A by 18:00. If he departs from C at 16:00 at 2 m/s find

   a the distance and bearing of Raphael's journey from C to A

   b if Raphael arrives back at village A by 18:00.

10 The centre of a clock face is 30 m above the ground. The hour hand is 1.5 m long. Find the height of the hour hand above the ground at 21:30.

11 A firework travels vertically for 100 m, then for 75 m at 20° to the vertical, then 50 m at 20° to the horizontal. It then drops vertically to the ground in 1 minute.
Find the average speed of its descent in m/s.

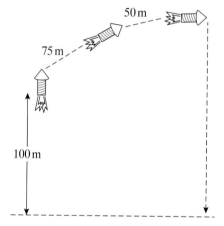

12 A ship 5 km North of an oil-rig travels on a bearing of 150°. Calculate the closest distance that the ship passes by the oil-rig.

13 A large fun-fair swing consists of a 5 m chain at the end of which is the seat. Find how far above the lowest point the seat is when the chain makes an angle of 50° with the vertical.

14 A regular hexagon is inscribed inside a circle of radius 10 m.
What percentage of the circle is taken up by the hexagon?

Handling data 3

Calculation of averages using frequency tables

Exercise 15

For each question in this exercise copy out the table of data.

1 At a fair, Toby fires an air rifle at a target. The table shows the information about his scores.

   a How many times did he fire at the target?

   b Find his median score.

   c Find the mode of his scores.

   d Calculate his mean score.

Score	Frequency
0	8
1	4
2	5
4	2
6	1

2 The table shows the number of appointments patients made with a doctor last week.

   a How many patients made appointments?

   b Find the median number of appointments per patient.

   c Find the mode of the number of appointments per patient.

   d Calculate the mean number of appointments per patient.

Number of appointments	Frequency
1	16
2	12
3	7
4	4
5	1

3 Alice is amusing herself by counting the number of times her Maths teacher says "Um" during a lesson. The table shows her results for a term.

   a How many Maths lessons did Alice have during the term?

   b Write down the modal class.

   c Calculate an estimate for the mean number of "Um"s per lesson.

Number of "Um"s	Frequency
1–5	3
6–10	7
11–15	14
16–20	16
21–25	10

4 As part of her routine examination a vet weighs every cat she sees in her surgery. The table shows her results for a week.

   a How many cats did she see that week?

   b Write down the modal class.

   c Calculate an estimate of the mean weight of these cats.

Weight (w kg)	Number of cats
$0 < w \leqslant 2$	2
$2 < w \leqslant 4$	6
$4 < w \leqslant 6$	10
$6 < w \leqslant 8$	5
$8 < w \leqslant 10$	1

5 The times of some cross-country runners in a race are given in the table.

a How many runners took part in the race?

b Write down the modal class.

c Calculate an estimate of the mean time of these runners.

Time (t mins)	Frequency
11.5 < t ≤ 14.5	3
14.5 < t ≤ 17.5	7
17.5 < t ≤ 20.5	11
20.5 < t ≤ 23.5	4

6 The table shows information about the ages of students who sing in the choir.

a How many students sing in the choir?

b Write down the modal class.

c Calculate the mean of these ages.

d Another student joins the choir on her 13th birthday. Will the mean increase or decrease? Give a reason for your answer.

Age (a years)	Frequency
12 ≤ a < 13	8
13 ≤ a < 14	5
14 ≤ a < 15	9
15 ≤ a < 16	6
16 ≤ a < 17	4

Exercise 15★

For each question in this exercise copy out the table of data.

1 Fifty people took part in a golf tournament. The table shows the scores.

a How many people scored 72?

b Find the median score.

c Find the mode of the scores.

d Calculate the mean score.

Score	Frequency
70	2
71	5
72	
73	11
74	15
75	9

2 The table shows the number of children in some families. The mean number of children per family is 2.2.

a Calculate the value of x.

b Find the median number of children per family.

c What percentage of families have less than two children?

Number of children	Number of families
0	2
1	6
2	11
3	x
4	3
5	1

3 Each day for a month Ross keeps a record of the number of calls he makes on his mobile phone. The table shows the results.

a In which month did Ross do his survey?

b Write down the modal class interval.

c Work out an estimate of the mean number of calls per day.

Number of calls	Frequency
1–5	2
6–10	4
11–15	7
16–20	9
21–25	6

4 The table shows the number of words in some essays written in an English exam.

a How many students took the exam?

b Write down the modal class interval.

c Calculate an estimate of the mean number of words per essay.

Number of words	Number of essays
401–600	150
601–800	425
801–1000	350
1001–1200	75

5 A Monro is the name given to any mountain in Scotland over 3000 feet in height. The table shows the distribution of Monros by height.

a How many Monros are there in Scotland?

b Write down the modal class interval.

c Calculate an estimate of the mean height of a Monro, giving your answer to the nearest ten feet.

Height (h feet)	Frequency
$3000 < h \leqslant 3300$	300
$3300 < h \leqslant 3600$	135
$3600 < h \leqslant 3900$	80
$3900 < h \leqslant 4200$	20
$4200 < h \leqslant 4500$	5

6 The table shows the maximum speed of serve of 50 players in a professional tennis tournament.

a What value, in terms of x, should go in the blank space in the frequency column of the table?

The calculation of the estimate of the mean speed gave the result 107.8 mph.

b Calculate the value of x.

Speed (s mph)	Frequency
$90 < s \leqslant 100$	x
$100 < s \leqslant 110$	23
$110 < s \leqslant 120$	
$120 < s \leqslant 130$	5

1 a £1500 is invested for 4 years at 7% compound interest. Calculate the interest earned.

  b £1500 is invested for 7 years at 4% compound interest. Calculate the interest earned.

2 The population of a tropical island is increasing at the rate of 3.5% per year. How long will it take for the population to double?

3 An antique glass bowl was valued at £10,000 at the end of 1998. This value increased by 25% in 1999 and by 22% in 2000. Its value fell by 30% in 2001. What was its value on January 1st 2002?

4 Light travels at 2.998×10^8 m/s. Calculate an estimate of how far light travels in a year. Give your answer, correct to 3 significant figures, in km, using standard form.

5 a Calculate the value of $\dfrac{2.94^2}{34.9 + 67.1} + \dfrac{0.0089}{1.2}$, writing down the full calculator display.

  b Give the answer to 3 significant figures, in standard form.

6 Find the highest common factor and lowest common mulitple of 12 and 30.

7 Simplify these algebraic expressions.

  a $\dfrac{30}{xy^2} \div \dfrac{6x^2}{x^2y}$ b $\dfrac{x+1}{7} - \dfrac{x-3}{21}$

8 Solve the equation $\dfrac{2(x+1)}{5} - \dfrac{3(x+1)}{10} = x$

9 Solve these simultaneous equations. $4x - 3y = 26$

                                       $2x + y + 10 = 0$

10 XYZ is an obtuse-angled triangle. Point P is the foot of the perpendicular from Y onto XZ produced. XY = 10 cm, XZ = 4 cm, Angle PXY = 40° Calculate

  a length YP

  b length XP

  c length ZP

  d angle PZY

  e angle XZY

  f area of triangle XYZ.

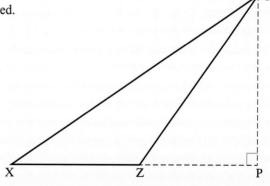

11 Find the sides x and z and the angle y.

a

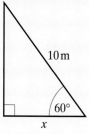

10 m

60°

x

b

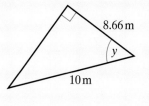

8.66 m

y

10 m

c

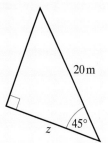

20 m

45°

z

12 Find the angle x and the side y.

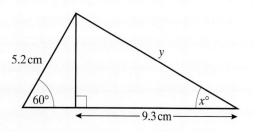

5.2 cm

y

60°

$x°$

9.3 cm

13 The bar chart shows the goals scored per game by Liverpool FC

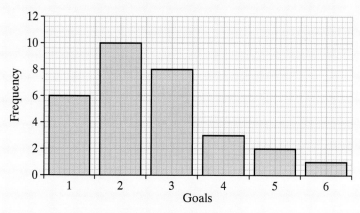

Calculate the mean number of goals scored per game.

14 The number of goals scored in a hockey season by Gabi is shown in the table.

No. of goals x	Frequency f	fx
0	12	
1	14	
2	16	
3	6	
4	2	
	$\Sigma f =$	$\Sigma fx =$

a Copy and complete the table to find the sum of all the goals scored by Gabi.

b Find the mean number of goals Gabi scored per game.

15 The delayed times of trains at La Gare du Nord, Paris, on Jan 1st 2006 are shown in the table:

Delay d (mins)	Mid-point x	No. of trains f	fx
$0 \leqslant d < 30$		10	
$30 \leqslant d < 60$		14	
$60 \leqslant d < 90$		16	
$90 \leqslant d < 120$		11	
$120 \leqslant d < 150$		8	
$150 \leqslant d < 180$		1	
		$\Sigma f =$	$\Sigma fx =$

a Copy and complete the table to find the total number of delayed trains.

b Use this value to estimate the mean delay of these trains.

c Why is this value only an estimate?

Number 4

Inverse percentages, upper and lower bounds, rounding and estimating

Exercise 16

1 Ali sells her goat for $150, giving her a profit of 25%. Find the original price she paid for the goat.

2 Liam sells a bag of rice for $24, giving him a profit of 20%. Find the original price he paid for the rice.

3 Pierre sells an oil painting for £2125, giving him a loss of 15%. Find the original price he paid for the painting.

4 Guvinda ran 400 m in 77.6 seconds which was an improvement of 3%. Find her original time.

5 If $w = \dfrac{ac}{b}$, and $a = 2.5 \pm 0.1$, $b = 3.5 \pm 0.1$ and $c = 4.5 \pm 0.1$, calculate correct to 3 significant figures the maximum and minimum values of w.

6 If $x = \dfrac{a + b}{c}$, and $a = 5.5 \pm 0.3$, $b = 3.5 \pm 0.5$ and $c = 2.5 \pm 0.1$, calculate correct to 3 significant figures the maximum and minimum values of x.

7 If $y = \dfrac{a + b}{c - d}$, and $a = 1.5 \pm 0.1$, $b = 2.5 \pm 0.1$, $c = 5.5 \pm 0.1$ and $d = 3.5 \pm 0.1$ calculate correct to 3 significant figures the maximum and minimum values of y.

8 If $z = \dfrac{a - b}{c + d}$, and $a = 10.5 \pm 0.1$, $b = 2.5 \pm 0.1$, $c = 1.5 \pm 0.1$ and $d = 3.5 \pm 0.1$, calculate correct to 3 significant figures the maximum and minimum values of z.

For Questions 9–20, make an estimate of the following correct to 1 significant figure in standard form:

9 $(1.9 \times 10^3) \times (5.1 \times 10^4)$

10 $(4.9 \times 10^7) \times (8.1 \times 10^5)$

11 $(6.8 \times 10^6) \times (7.9 \times 10^8)$

12 $(1.1 \times 10^6) \times (9.9 \times 10^4)$

13 $(7.9 \times 10^5) \div (4.1 \times 10^3)$

14 $(3.9 \times 10^7) \div (1.8 \times 10^4)$

15 $(8.9 \times 10^9) \div (1.9 \times 10^2)$

16 $(9.7 \times 10^{12}) \div (1.9 \times 10^4)$

17 $18\,000\,000 \times 19\,000\,000$

18 $49\,000 \times 61\,000\,000\,000$

19 $21\,800\,000 \div 19\,700$

20 $79\,950\,000\,000\,000 \div 3\,900$

Exercise 16★

1 A valuable clock has an original price of x. It is sold for $5000 after its original price has been increased by 5% and then by 10%. Find x.

2 A stone garden statue has an original price of €y. It is sold for €2500 after its original price has been increased by 15% and then by 20%. Find y.

3 A doll's house has an original price of £x. It is sold for £350 after its original price has been decreased by 5% and then by 10%. Find x.

4 A mountain bike has an original price of £y. It is sold for £1750 after its original price has been decreased by 15% and then by 20%. Find y.

5 An antique chair has an original price of p. It is sold for $1250 after its original price has been increased by 7% and then decreased by 9%. Find p.

6 An exclusive apartment in New York has a value of q. It is sold for $1 million after its original price decreases by 10% and then increases by 25%. Find q.

7 A pearl necklace has a value of €7500 after it has appreciated by 3% per year for 3 years. Find its original value 3 years ago.

8 A signed shirt by a world famous footballer has a value of £1800 after it has depreciated by 5% per year for 5 years. Find its original value 5 years ago.

9 If $w = \sqrt{\frac{a^2 - b^2}{\pi c}}$, and $a = 7.5 \pm 0.1$, $b = 1.5 \pm 0.1$ and $c = 3.5 \pm 0.1$ calculate, correct to 3 significant figures, the maximum and minimum values of w.

10 If $w = \left(\frac{a}{b - c}\right)^3$ and $a = 2.5 \pm 0.1$, $b = 8.5 \pm 0.1$ and $c = 3.5 \pm 0.1$ calculate, correct to 3 significant figures, the maximum and minimum values of w.

11 If $y = \frac{10\sin a}{b - c}$, and $a = 30° \pm 0.5°$, $b = 2.9 \pm 0.1$ and $c = 1.2 \pm 0.1$ calculate, correct to 3 significant figures, the maximum and minimum values of y.

12 A circular persian rug has a diameter of 4 m to the nearest metre. Find, to 3 significant figures, the greatest and least
  a area
  b perimeter.

For Questions 13–18, make an estimate of the following correct to 1 significant figure in standard form.

13 $0.005\,912 \times 290\,000\,000$

14 $0.000\,007\,987 \div 0.001\,967$

15 $(3.89 \times 10^{-7}) \times (5.91 \times 10^{-6})$

16 $4\,890\,000\,000 \times 0.000\,9$

17 $(5.81 \times 10^{-5}) \div (2.98 \times 10^{-6})$

18 $(7.71 \times 10^{-3}) + (3.98 \times 10^{-4})$

Algebra 4

Rearranging equations and using formulae

Exercise 17

Make x the subject of these equations.

1 $x + 1 = a$

2 $x - a = 1$

3 $b = x + a$

4 $3x = a$

5 $bx = a$

6 $2x + b = a$

7 $bx + 2 = a$

8 $a - 3x = b$

9 $3(a + x) = b$

10 $\frac{ax}{2} = b$

11 $3x^2 = a$

12 $\frac{x^2}{3} = a$

13 $x^2 + 3 = a$

14 $x^2 - 3 = a$

15 $2x^2 + 3 = a$

16 $2(x^2 + 3) = a$

17 $3\sqrt{x} = a$

18 $\sqrt{x} - 3 = a$

19 $\frac{\sqrt{x}}{3} = a$

20 $2x - a = x + b$

21 The speed v m/s of a racing car t seconds after exiting a corner in a race is given by $v = 20 + 5t$.

    a Find the speed of the car after 5 seconds.

    b Make t the subject of the formula.

    c Find how long it takes the car to reach 30 m/s.

22 A shop finds that the number, N, of ice-creams it sells is related to the temperature T °C by the formula $N = 150 + 2.5T$ for $20 \leqslant T \leqslant 30$.

    a Find N when T is 22.

    b Make T the subject of the formula.

    c Find T if $N = 220$.

23 The surface area, A, of a spherical ball of radius r is given by the formula $A = 4\pi r^2$.

    a Find the surface area of a football with radius 10.5 cm.

    b Make r the subject of the formula.

    c A tennis ball has a surface area of 201 cm². Find the radius.

24 The diagram shows a pattern of shapes made from cubes of side 1 cm.

   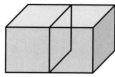   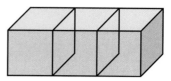

Shape number 1   Shape number 2   Shape number 3

A rule to find the surface area of a shape in this pattern is
    "Multiply the shape number by two, add one and then multiply your answer by two"
A is the surface area of shape number n.

a Find and simplify a formula for A in terms of n.

b Find A when $n = 100$.

c Make n the subject of your formula in part **a**.

d What shape number has a surface area of $214\,\text{cm}^2$?

Exercise 17★

Make x the subject of these equations.

1 $x - a = b$

2 $ax - b = c$

3 $ax = b$

4 $\dfrac{ax}{b} = c$

5 $a(x - b) = c$

6 $a(b - x) = c$

7 $\dfrac{x}{a} + b = c$

8 $\dfrac{x + b}{a} = c$

9 $\dfrac{a - b}{x} = c$

10 $\dfrac{a}{x} + b = c$

11 $ax^2 = b$

12 $\dfrac{x^2}{a} = b$

13 $a(x^2 - b) = c$

14 $\dfrac{x^2}{a} - b = c$

15 $\dfrac{a}{x^2} = b$

16 $a\sqrt{x} - b = c$

17 $a(\sqrt{x} - b) = c$

18 $ax = x + b$

19 $a(x + 1) = b(1 - x)$

20 $\dfrac{x + a}{x + b} = 2$

21 A formula to find the number, N, of rolls of wallpaper needed to wallpaper a room with wall area $A\,\text{m}^2$ is given by $N = 2 + 0.4A$.

a A room measures 5 m long by 4 m wide by 2.5 m high. Find the number of rolls required to wallpaper this room, ignoring any windows or doors.

b Make A the subject of the formula.

c Find A if $N = 30$.

22 Vicky is pushing her baby daughter on a swing. The time, t seconds, to complete one swing is given

by $t = 2\pi\sqrt{\dfrac{l}{10}}$ where l m is the length of the swing.

a Find t if $l = 2$ m

b Make l the subject of the formula.

c Find l if $t = 2.5$ seconds.

23 The cost, £C, of each ticket for a concert is given by $C = 10 + \dfrac{200}{n}$ where n is the number of people buying a ticket.

a Find C when $n = 50$.

b Make n the subject of the formula.

c Find n if the cost of each ticket is £11.25.

24 The surface area, A cm^2, of a cylindrical drinks can with height h cm and radius r cm is given by $A = 2\pi r(r + h)$.

a Find the surface area of a coke can with $h = 11$ cm and $r = 3.25$ cm.

b Make h the subject of the formula.

c Another can has $A = 500$ cm^2 and $r = 4$ cm. Find the value of h.

Graphs 4

Quadratic graphs

Exercise 18

For Questions 1–6, draw a graph for each equation after compiling a suitable table for $-3 \leqslant x \leqslant 3$.

1 $y = x^2 + 1$

2 $y = x^2 - 1$

3 $y = 2x^2 + 1$

4 $y = 2x^2 - 1$

5 $y = x^2 + x$

6 $y = x^2 - x$

For Questions 7–10, copy and complete the tables, then draw the graph.

7 $y = x^2 + x + 3$

x	-2	-1	0	1	2	3
y	5		3			

8 $y = x^2 + x - 5$

x	-2	-1	0	1	2	3
y			-5	-3		

9 $y = x^2 + 2x + 7$

x	-3	-2	-1	0	1	2	3	4
y			6		10			

10 $y = x^2 + 3x - 4$

x	-3	-2	-1	0	1	2	3	4
y			6		0			

11 Draw the graph of $y = x^2 - x - 2$ for $-3 \leqslant x \leqslant 3$ and use this graph to solve the equation $0 = x^2 - x - 2$.

12 Draw the graph of $y = x^2 + x - 6$ for $-4 \leqslant x \leqslant 4$ and use this graph to solve the equation $0 = x^2 + x - 6$.

13 Draw the graph of $y = x^2 - 2x - 8$ for $-3 \leqslant x \leqslant 5$ and use this graph to solve the equation $0 = x^2 - 2x - 8$.

14 The distance y m fallen by a free-falling parachutist t seconds after jumping out of an aeroplane is given by the equation $y = 5t^2$.

    a Draw the graph of y against t for $0 \leqslant t \leqslant 5$.

    b Use your graph to estimate:

        i The distance fallen after 3.5 s.

        ii The number of seconds it takes the parachutist to fall 25 m.

Exercise 18★

For Questions 1–4, draw a graph for each equation after compiling a suitable table between the stated x values.

1 $y = 2x^2 - 3x - 4$ $-3 \leqslant x \leqslant 3$ **2** $y = -2x^2 + 3x + 4$ $-3 \leqslant x \leqslant 3$

3 $y = (x + 3)(2x - 5)$ $-4 \leqslant x \leqslant 4$ **4** $y = (2x - 3)^2$ $0 \leqslant x \leqslant 4$

5 The partially completed table for $y = 2x^2 - 7x + p$ is shown below.

x	0	1	2	3	4	5
y	5					

    a By making a suitable substitution for x, find the value of p.

    b Copy and complete the table and draw the graph.

    c Use the graph to solve the equation $2x^2 - 7x + p = 0$.

6 The partially completed table for $y = 2x^2 + px + q$ is shown below.

x	-2	-1	0	1	2	3	4
y			-3				13

    a By making suitable substitutions for x find the values of p and q.

    b Copy and complete the table and draw the graph.

    c Use the graph to solve the equation $2x^2 + px + q = 0$.

7 The profit p (£1000s) made by a new coffee shop Caffeine Rush, t months after opening, is given by the equation $p = 10t - kt^2$, valid for $0 \leqslant t \leqslant 4$, where k is a constant.

    a Use this table to find the value of k, and then copy and complete the table.

t	0	1	2	3	4
p		7			

    b Draw the graph of p against t.

    c Use it to estimate

        i The greatest profit made by Caffeine Rush and when it occurred.

        ii When Caffeine Rush starts to make a loss.

8 Consider the graph of $y = px^2 + qx + r$ where p, q and r are integers.

    Sketch the following graphs if

    a $p > 0, q = 0$ and $r > 0$ **b** $p > 0, q = 0$ and $r < 0$

    c $p = 0, q > 0$ and $r > 0$ **d** $p < 0, q = 0$ and $r > 0$.

Shape and space 4

Circles, similar triangles and Pythagoras' theorem

Exercise 19

For Questions 1–12 find the size of each lettered angle.

1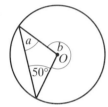

2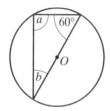

3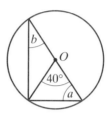

4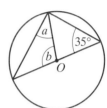

5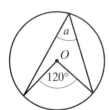

6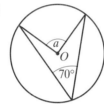

7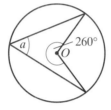

8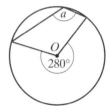

9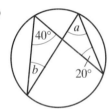

10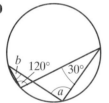

11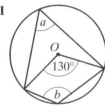

12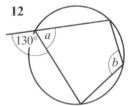

13 The two triangles are similar.
Calculate *a* and *b*.

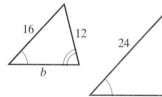

14 Calculate *a*.

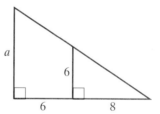

15 Calculate *a* and *b*.

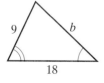

16 Calculate *a* and *b*.

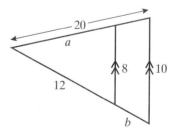

17 Calculate *a*.

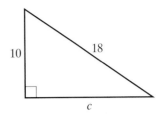

18 Calculate *b*.

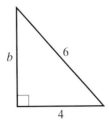

19 Calculate *c*.

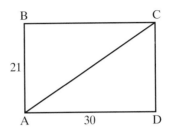

20 ABCD is a rectangular piece of paper.
Find the length AC.

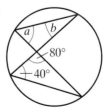

Exercise 19★

For Questions 1–12 find the size of each lettered angle.

1

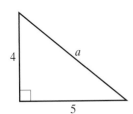

2

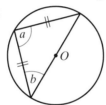

3

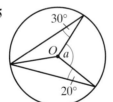

4

5

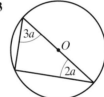

6

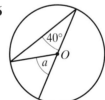

7

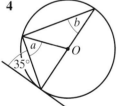

8

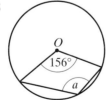

9

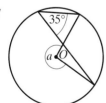

10

11

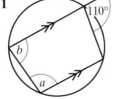

12

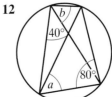

13 Calculate *a*.

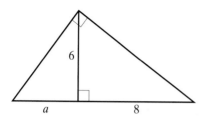

14 Calculate *a* and *b*.

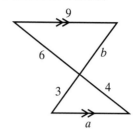

15 Calculate *a* and *b*.

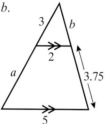

16 a Show that the two triangles are similar.

   b Calculate *a* and *b*.

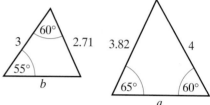

17 Calculate *a*.

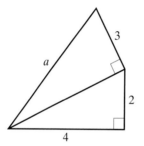

18 Calculate *a*.

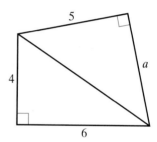

19 a Calculate the radius of the circle

   b Calculate *a*.

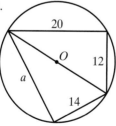

20 The diagram shows a circle with radius 5 cm.
   AB = 8 cm and X is the
   midpoint of AB

   Find **a** XC   **b** AC.

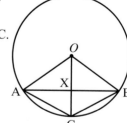

Handling data 4

Single event probability

Exercise 20

1 Gita wishes to estimate her probability of scoring a goal in hockey from a penalty.
She does this by taking 10 penalties in succession, with the following results.
Score: S   Miss: M
S S M M M S S S M S
Use a relative frequency diagram to estimate the probability of scoring.

2 The probability of it snowing in New York on Dec 25th is 0.2.
What is the probability of New York not experiencing a 'White Christmas'?

3 A box contains twelve roses. Four are white, two are red and six are pink.
Sacha picks out one rose at random. What is the probability that it is

  a pink   **b** not red

  c white, red or pink   **d** yellow?

4 One letter is randomly chosen from this sentence.
'I have hardly ever known a mathematician who was capable of reasoning'.
What is the probability of the letter being

  a an 'e'   **b** an 'a'

  c a consonant (non-vowel)   **d** a 'z'?

5 Jamal receives 50 e-mails. 32 are from England, 12 are from the U.S.A. and the rest are from China.
He chooses one at random to read first. What is the probability that it is from

  a France   **b** the U.S.A. or China

  c England   **d** not England?

6 A card is randomly selected from a pack of 52 playing cards. Calculate the probability that it is

  a a Queen   **b** a King or a Jack

  c not a heart   **d** a red picture card.

7 A fair eight-sided die has numbered faces from 1 to 8. After it is thrown, find the probability of obtaining a

  a 3   **b** prime number

  c a number of at least 3   **d** a number of at most 5.

8 A fair six-sided die is cast 120 times. How many times would you expect to roll a multiple of three?

9 A box contains a red marble and three green marbles. Two are taken at random.

  a Write down all the possible outcomes in a table.

  b Use this table to find the probability of obtaining one marble of each colour.

10 Zak decides to guess each answer in a Physics multiple choice test. There are 20 questions, each with four options A, B, C and D. How many questions should Zak expect to get right?

Exercise 20 ★

1 Two fair six-sided dice are thrown and their scores are multiplied.

   a Write down all the possible outcomes in a table.

   b Use this table to find the probability of the following scores being obtained.

      i 36   **ii** 11   **iii** a multiple of 5   **iv** at least 20.

2 Three discs are in a black box and are numbered 10, 30 and 50. Four discs are in a white box and these are numbered 9, 16, 25 and 36. Two discs, one from each box are randomly selected and the *highest* number of the two scores is noted.

   a Construct a suitable 'probability space' table.

   b Use this table to find the probability of the following scores being obtained.

      i 10   **ii** a prime number   **iii** an even number   **iv** a square number.

3 Three vets record the number of horses which are cured after being given a particular medicine.

Vet	Number of horses given medicine	Number of horses cured
Mr Stamp	18	16
Mrs Khan	14	11
Miss Abu	10	9

Calculate the probability that

   a a horse given the medicine by Mr Stamp or Miss Abu will be cured.

   b a horse given the medicine by Mrs Khan or Miss Abu will not be cured.

   c all three vets treat 714 horses in total with this medicine. How many would you expect not to be cured?

4 Baby Kiera has two toy boxes. The pink box contains a triangle, a circle and a star whilst the blue box contains a square, a rectangle and a star. She randomly picks one shape from each box to play with. She is happy as long as at least one of these shapes is a star.

   a Construct a suitable 'probability space' table.

   b Use this table to find the probability that:

      i Kiera is happy   **ii** Kiera is not happy.

5 A garden pond contains 40 Koi Carp, of which x are golden and the others are white. If 20 more golden Koi Carp are added to the pond, the probability of catching a golden Koi Carp is doubled. Find x.

6 Liam buys eight raffle tickets from 250 sold. If he does not win anything from any of the first five tickets drawn, find the probability that he will win on the sixth draw.

Examination practice 4

1 A Mini motor car is sold for £12 500 after it has depreciated by 12.5% from brand new. Find the original purchase price.

2 A valuable stone sculpture is purchased for €25 000 after it has appreciated by 10%. Find the original price.

3 **Without a calculator** and showing your working, use standard form to calculate an **estimate** of

   a $\dfrac{497 + 33}{0.000802}$ **b** $\sqrt{2.62 \times 10^5}$

4 The area of a circle is given as $45.5 \pm 0.5\,\text{cm}^2$. Find, correct to 3 significant figures, the maximum possible radius and minimum possible circumference.

5 Make x the subject of this equation.

   $V = \dfrac{ab - x}{g}$

6 Make x the subject of this equation.

   $a(x - b) = c(d - x)$

7 Make x the subject of this equation.

   $P = \dfrac{\sqrt{x + Q}}{R}$

8 Draw the graph of

   a $y = 2x^2 - 3x - 1$ for $-2 \leqslant x \leqslant 3$ and use it to solve the equation $2x^2 - 3x - 1 = 0$.

   b $y = -2x^2 + 3x + 1$ for $-2 \leqslant x \leqslant 3$ and use it to solve the equation $-2x^2 + 3x + 1 = 0$.

9 Find the value of the lettered sides of these right-angled triangles.

   a
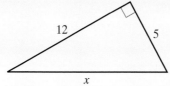
   b
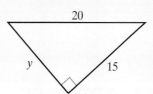

10 Find the distance between the points A(4, −3) and B(12, 6).

11 Find sides x and y.

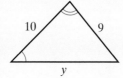

12 Find sides x and y.

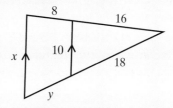

For Questions 13–16 find the size of each lettered angle.

13

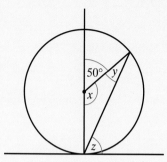

14

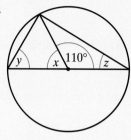

15

16

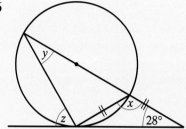

17 Two fair six-sided dice are rolled and the outcomes are added together.

   a Draw a probability space diagram showing all possible outcomes.

   b Calculate the probability that the sum will be

     i 10

     ii a multiple of 5

     iii not 7

     iv 15.

18 A letter is chosen randomly from a collection of Scrabble tiles that spell the expression TRIGONOMETRICAL CALCULATION. Calculate the probability that it is

   a an O   **b** an L

   c a vowel   **d** an E or a consonant.

19 Three fair coins are tossed at the same time.

   a Write down all the possible outcomes in a probability space table.

   b Find the probability of obtaining

     i three heads   **ii** two heads   **iii** at least one tail.

20 The formula for t is given by $t = \left(\dfrac{1 + e}{1 - e}\right)\sqrt{\dfrac{h}{5}}$

   a Make e the subject of the formula.

   b Calculate the value of e when $t = 2.5$ and $h = 1.25$.

Number 5

Proportion and recurring decimals

Exercise 21

Express these recurring decimals as fractions in their simplest terms.

1 $0.\dot{1}$ 2 $0.\dot{2}$ 3 $0.\dot{3}$

4 $0.\dot{3}\dot{6}$ 5 $0.\dot{6}\dot{3}$ 6 $0.\dot{1}\dot{7}$

7 $0.\dot{7}\dot{1}$ 8 $0.\dot{9}$ 9 $0.\dot{1}\dot{2}$

10 $0.\dot{3}\dot{4}$ 11 $0.\dot{5}\dot{6}$ 12 $0.\dot{6}\dot{7}$

13 $0.\dot{7}\dot{8}$ 14 $0.0\dot{8}\dot{9}$ 15 $0.0\dot{9}\dot{1}$

16 Convert $10\,\text{m/s}$ to km/h.

17 Convert $10\,\text{km/h}$ to m/s.

18 Which curry powder is the better value:
Jar A: 125 g at £3.75, or Jar B: 75 g at £2.25 ?

19 Which wall tiles are the better value:
Square: $10\,\text{m}^2$ for €250, or
Octagonal: $25\,\text{m}^2$ for €600?

20 Which 12 volt battery is the better value:
Everamp, for £3.60 which last 72 hours, or
Dynamo, for £5.25 which last 126 hours ?

21 Which mobile phone company gives better value for 24 hours of calls:
Tangerine; one phone costing $25 and a line rate of $0.35/min.
Aardvark; one phone costing $40 and a line rate of $0.30/min ?

22 A light-year is the length a light particle travels in an Earth year. Given that the speed of light is 299 792 458 m/s, find the length of a light-year in mm. Give your answer in standard form correct to 3 significant figures.

23 Oak has a density of $0.7\,\text{g/cm}^3$. Find the mass in kg, of an oak door measuring $2.2\,\text{m} \times 0.9\,\text{m} \times 0.05\,\text{m}$.

24 A garden pond has a volume of $50\,\text{m}^3$. Given that water has a density of $1\,\text{g/cm}^3$ find the mass of the water in the pond in kg.

25 If gold has a density of $19.9\,\text{g/cm}^3$ and a price of £10 250 per kg, find the value of a gold statue of volume $100\,\text{cm}^3$.

Exercise 21 ★

Express these recurring decimals as fractions in their simplest terms.

1 $0.0\dot{2}$

2 $0.0\dot{7}$

3 $0.07\dot{5}$

4 $0.1\dot{2}\dot{3}$

5 $0.1\dot{2}3\dot{4}$

6 $0.\dot{2}46\dot{8}$

7 $0.7\dot{3}$

8 $0.3\dot{7}$

9 $0.001\dot{7}$

10 $0.023\dot{4}$

For Questions 11−16 use this currency conversion table.

Country	Currency	Rate/£1.00
Australia	Dollars	2.51
Brazil	Reais	4.19
China	Yuan	15.28
India	Rupees	86.72
Malaysia	Ringitts	6.87
Russia	Rubles	52.12
USA	Dollars	1.96

11 Convert 1000 rubles into British pounds.

12 Convert 1000 rupees into Australian dollars.

13 Convert 500 yuan into Malaysian ringitts.

14 Nicki travels from the UK to three countries: Malaysia, India and China.
She has £3600 to convert and wishes to do so in the ratio of 1 : 2 : 3 for each country respectively.
How much of each currency will she have for each stage of her journey?

15 Kristal High Definition TVs cost the following in different countries:

Australia	3765 Dollars
Brazil	5866 Reais
USA	$2450

Convert each price into British pounds and state which country sells this high definition TV most cheaply.

16 In 2005 the world had a birth toll of 129 908 352 babies, whilst the number of deaths in the same year was 56 622 744. Calculate

a the change in the world population in 2005

b The change in the world population per second.

c The birth rate in 2005 per second.

d the death rate in 2005 per second.

Algebra 5

Expanding brackets, factorising and solving quadratic equations

Exercise 22

Multiply out and simplify these expressions

1 $(x + 3)(x + 4)$ **2** $(x + 1)(x + 7)$ **3** $(x - 3)(x + 2)$

4 $(x + 6)(x - 1)$ **5** $(x - 4)(x - 2)$ **6** $(x + 1)^2$

7 $(x - 2)^2$ **8** $(x + 2)(x - 2)$ **9** $(2x + 1)(x + 2)$

10 $(3x - 1)(x + 3)$

Factorise these expressions.

11 $x^2 + 3x$ **12** $x^2 - 2x$ **13** $x^2 + x$

14 $x^2 - 4x$ **15** $x^2 - 4$ **16** $x^2 - 36$

17 $x^2 + 7x + 12$ **18** $x^2 + x - 12$ **19** $x^2 - x - 12$

20 $x^2 - 7x + 12$ **21** $x^2 + 8x + 12$ **22** $x^2 - 4x - 12$

23 $x^2 + 4x - 12$ **24** $x^2 - 8x + 12$ **25** $x^2 + 13x + 12$

26 $x^2 + 11x - 12$ **27** $x^2 - 13x + 12$ **28** $x^2 - 11x - 12$

Solve these quadratic equations.

29 $(x + 1)(x + 3) = 0$ **30** $(x - 1)(x + 2) = 0$ **31** $(x + 4)(x - 3) = 0$

32 $(x - 1)(x - 2) = 0$ **33** $(x - 2)^2 = 0$ **34** $(x + 4)^2 = 0$

35 $x(x + 7) = 0$ **36** $x(x - 5) = 0$ **37** $0 = (x + 2)(x - 4)$

38 $0 = (3 - x)(x + 5)$

Solve these quadratic equations.

39 $x^2 + 3x + 2 = 0$ **40** $x^2 + 4x + 3 = 0$ **41** $x^2 + 3x - 4 = 0$

42 $x^2 - 4x + 3 = 0$ **43** $x^2 - 6x + 5 = 0$ **44** $x^2 + x - 6 = 0$

45 $x^2 - 5x + 6 = 0$ **46** $x^2 + 5x - 6 = 0$ **47** $x^2 - 6x + 8 = 0$

48 $x^2 + 2x + 1 = 0$ **49** $x^2 - 4 = 0$ **50** $x^2 - 25 = 0$

51 $x^2 + 2x = 0$ **52** $x^2 - 4x = 0$

53 A coconut falls from the top of a 20 m high palm tree. After t seconds the coconut has fallen a distance of x m where $x = 5t^2$. Find how long, in seconds, it takes for the coconut to hit the ground.

54 The rectangle and the square have the same area. Find the value of x.

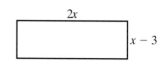

55 A rectangular carpet has a length of $(x + 2)$ m and a width of x m.
  a Write down and simplify an expression for the area of the carpet.
  b If the area is 15 m², find the value of x.

Exercise 22★

Multiply out and simplify these expressions.

1 $(x + 8)(x + 3)$ **2** $(x - 5)(x + 2)$

3 $(x - 7)(x + 7)$ **4** $(x + 8)^2$

5 $(x - 5)^2$ **6** $(x - 9)(x + 9)$

7 $(2x + 1)(3x + 1)$ **8** $(4x - 3)(2x + 2)$

9 $(3x + 5)(3x - 5)$ **10** $(5x - 4)^2$

Factorise these expressions.

11 $x^2 + 49x$ **12** $x^2 - 144x$ **13** $x^2 - 49$

14 $x^2 - 144$ **15** $2x^2 - 72$ **16** $3x^2 - 48$

17 $x^2 + 10x + 24$ **18** $x^2 - 10x + 24$ **19** $x^2 - 2x - 24$

20 $x^2 + 11x + 24$ **21** $x^2 - 5x - 24$ **22** $x^2 - 11x + 24$

23 $x^2 + 14x + 24$ **24** $x^2 - 14x + 24$ **25** $x^2 + 10x - 24$

26 $x^2 + 25x + 24$ **27** $x^2 + 23x - 24$ **28** $x^2 - 23x - 24$

Solve these quadratic equations.

29 $(x - 11)(x + 5) = 0$ **30** $(x + 7)(x + 2) = 0$

31 $(x - 5)^2 = 0$ **32** $x(x - 13) = 0$

33 $0 = (x - 6)(x - 3)$ **34** $(2 - x)(x + 5) = 0$

35 $(7 - x)(8 + x) = 0$ **36** $(2x - 6)(x + 1) = 0$

37 $(3x + 6)(4x - 12) = 0$ **38** $(2x - 1)(3x + 1) = 0$

Solve these quadratic equations by factorising.

39 $x^2 + 6x + 5 = 0$

40 $x^2 + 6x + 8 = 0$

41 $x^2 - 6x - 7 = 0$

42 $x^2 - 7x + 12 = 0$

43 $x^2 + 3x - 10 = 0$

44 $x^2 + 8x - 9 = 0$

45 $x^2 + 4x + 4 = 0$

46 $x^2 - 6x + 9 = 0$

47 $x^2 - 81 = 0$

48 $x^2 - 49 = 0$

49 $x^2 + 13x = 0$

50 $x^2 - 81x = 0$

51 $x^2 - 2x = 15$

52 $x^2 + x = 20$

53 The length of a photograph is 5 cm more than the width. Let the width be x cm.

   a Write down and simplify an expression for the area of the photograph.

   b If the area is 150 cm², find x.

54 Two integers differ by 6. The sum of the squares of these integers is 116. Find the two integers.

55 The stopping distance of a car travelling at x km/h is $\dfrac{x^2 + 30x}{150}$ metres.

   a A car takes 12 m to stop. Show that $x^2 + 30x = 1800$.

   b Find the value of x.

Sequences 5

Sequences and finding formula

Exercise 23

Find the next three numbers in these sequences.

1 1, 4, 7, 10, ...

2 $-11, -9, -7, -5, ...$

3 20, 16, 12, 8, ...

4 14, 11, 8, 5, ...

5 1, 4, 9, 16, ...

6 5, 7, 9, 11, 13, ...

7 1, 2, 4, 8, ...

8 1, 10, 100, 1000, ...

9 1024, 512, 256, 128, ...

10 1, 3, 6, 10, ...

Find the first three terms of these sequences.

11 nth term $= n + 1$

12 nth term $= n - 2$

13 nth term $= 2n + 3$

14 nth term $= 3n - 5$

15 nth term $= 5 - 3n$

16 nth term $= 2 - 2n$

17 nth term $= n^2 + 3$

18 nth term $= n^2 - 2$

19 nth term $= 4 + \dfrac{1}{n}$

20 nth term $= \dfrac{6}{n}$

Find the value of n for which the nth term has the value given in brackets.

21 nth term $= 2n + 5$ (29)

22 nth term $= 3n + 8$ (35)

23 nth term $= 5n - 12$ (23)

24 nth term $= 8n - 48$ (16)

25 nth term $= 13 - 2n$ (3)

26 nth term $= 26 - 4n$ (2)

27 nth term $= 4 + 1.5n$ (19)

28 nth term $= 3 - 0.5n$ (−1)

29 nth term $= n^2 + 1$ (17)

30 nth term $= n^2 - 7$ (29)

31 If the nth term $= 4n + 3$, which is the first term greater than 17?

32 If the nth term $= 3n - 7$, which is the first term greater than 25?

33 If the nth term $= 18 - 2n$, which is the first term less than 1?

34 If the nth term $= 13 - 5n$, which is the first term less than -4?

Find an expression, in terms of n, for the nth term of these sequences.

35 5, 6, 7, 8, ...

36 4, 6, 8, 10, ...

37 7, 11, 15, 19, ...

38 5, 8, 11, 14, ...

39 $-2, -1, 0, 1, ...$

40 $-5, -2, 1, 4, ...$

41 3, 2, 1, 0, ...

42 4, 2, 0, −2, ...

43 $-2, -3, -4, -5, ...$

44 $-5, -7, -9, -11, ...$

45 Tanya's pocket money in Euros per month, n months after her 14th birthday, is given by the sequence with nth term $30 + 2n$.

    a What is her pocket money after 6 months?

    b When does her pocket money equal €50?

    c How much extra pocket money does she get every month?

    d If Tanya's parents don't change this arrangement, how much money will Tanya get after 10 years?

46 Niko decides to start skipping to get fit. The number of skips he does n days after starting is given by the sequence with nth term $20 + 10n$.

    a Find the number of skips he does on the 20th day.

    b On which day does he do 100 skips?

    c How many extra skips is he doing each day?

    d How many skips will he do one year after starting?

Exercise 23★

Find the next three numbers in these sequences.

  1 8, 13, 18, 23, ...

  2 37, 29, 21, 13, ...

  3 1, 2.5, 4, 5.5, ...

  4 0.1, 0.4, 0.7, 1, ...

  5 10, 7.5, 5, 2.5, ...

  6 1, 3, 9, 27, ...

  7 1024, 256, 64, 16, ...

  8 1, −2, 4, −8, ...

  9 $2, 1, \frac{1}{2}, \frac{1}{4}, \dots$

  10 1, 1, 2, 3, 5, 8, ...

Find the first three terms of these sequences.

  11 nth term $= 5n + 3$

  12 nth term $= 4n - 7$

  13 nth term $= 11 - 6n$

  14 nth term $= \frac{n}{2} + 1$

  15 nth term $= n^2 - 4$

  16 nth term $= n^3 + 1$

  17 nth term $= n(n + 1)$

  18 nth term $= 2^n$

  19 nth term $= n + \frac{1}{n}$

  20 nth term $= \frac{4 - n}{n}$

Find the value of n for which the nth term has the value given in brackets.

  21 nth term $= 6n + 13$ (55)

  22 nth term $= 7n - 21$ (42)

  23 nth term $= 32 - 5n$ (2)

  24 nth term $= 18 - 11n$ (−15)

  25 nth term $= 1.5 + 2.5n$ (14)

  26 nth term $= 8.5 - 1.5n$ (−3.5)

  27 nth term $= n^2 - 8$ (136)

  28 nth term $= n^2 + 72$ (153)

  29 nth term $= \dfrac{24}{(n + 1)}$ (6)

  30 nth term $= 2 + \dfrac{1}{n}$ (2.2)

  31 If the nth term $= 5n - 12$, which is the first term greater than 82?

  32 If the nth term $= 52 - 17n$, which is the first term less than −30?

  33 If the nth term $= n^2 + 5$, which is the first term greater than 80?

  34 If the nth term $= \dfrac{1}{(n + 1)}$, which is the first term less than $\frac{1}{100}$?

Find an expression, in terms of n, for the nth term of these sequences.

35 5, 7, 9, 11, …

36 9, 13, 17, 21, …

37 −5, −2, 1, 4, …

38 1, 6, 11, 16, …

39 30, 34, 38, 42, …

40 18, 23, 28, 33, …

41 5, 3, 1, −1, …

42 1, −3, −7, −11, …

43 −7, −10, −13, −16, …

44 −11, −17, −23, −29, …

45 The weight in kilograms of a blue whale calf n days after birth is given by the sequence $3000 + 100n$ for $n \leqslant 200$.

   a Find the weight on the 10th day.

   b After how many days is the weight 18 tonnes?

   c What is the weight gain per day?

46 The world population n days after 1st January 2007 is given by the sequence with the rule $6.5 \times 10^9 + 1.8 \times 10^5 \times n$.

   a What is the increase per day?

   b What will the population be after one year?

   c When will the population first exceed 7 billion?

Shape and space 5

Transformations

Exercise 24

1 Find the image of point P(3, 4) after it has been
   a reflected in the x-axis
   b reflected in the y-axis
   c rotated about O by 90° in a clockwise direction
   d translated along vector $\begin{pmatrix} 7 \\ -6 \end{pmatrix}$.

2 Find the image of point Q(−3, 5) after it has been
   a reflected in y = 0
   b reflected in x = 0
   c rotated about O by +90°
   d translated along vector $\begin{pmatrix} -5 \\ 3 \end{pmatrix}$.

3 Draw the triangle ABC, where A is the point (1, 2), B is the point (1, 6) and C is the point (8, 2) on a
   set of axes where −8 ⩽ x ⩽ 16 and −8 ⩽ y ⩽ 10. Find the image of ABC after it has been
   a reflected in the x-axis
   b rotated about O by 90° in an anti-clockwise direction
   c translated along vector $\begin{pmatrix} -5 \\ 4 \end{pmatrix}$
   d enlarged by a scale factor of 2 about a centre of enlargement (0, 4).

4 a Reflect the flag F in the y-axis and label the
      image A.
   b Reflect A in the line y = x and label its image B.
   c Describe fully the single transformation which
      takes F to B.
   d Reflect A in the line x = 2; label this image C.
   e Describe the single transformation which takes
      F to C.

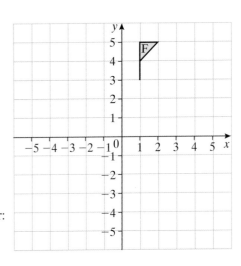

5 The image of a point P(x, y) is at point Q(4, 8) **after** P
   has undergone the following transformations in the order:

   Reflection in the x-axis.

   Rotation by 90° in a clockwise direction about O.

   Translation along vector $\begin{pmatrix} 3 \\ -3 \end{pmatrix}$.

   Find the value of x and y.

Exercise 24★

1 The image of triangle ABC is at J(2, 3), K(2, 5), L(6, 3) **after** it has undergone the following transformations in the order:

Reflection in the y-axis.

Rotation by 90° in an anti-clockwise direction about O.

Translation along vector $\begin{pmatrix} -3 \\ 4 \end{pmatrix}$.

Find the co-ordinates of triangle ABC.

2 a Triangle T undergoes the following transformations:

    i Reflection in the line $y = x$ after which the image is called A. Draw A.

    ii A 180° rotation about (1, 1) after which the image is called B. Draw B.

  b C is the image of B after a 180° rotation about (0, 2) after which the image is called C. Draw C.

  c Describe the single transformation that maps triangle A to triangle C.

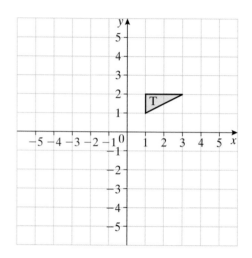

3 Triangle T is shown in the diagram.

  a T is reflected in line L to form image A. Draw triangle A.

  b A is reflected in $y = -1$ to form image B. Draw triangle B.

  c T undergoes a translation along vector $\begin{pmatrix} -2 \\ -3 \end{pmatrix}$ to form image C. Draw triangle C.

  d T is enlarged by a scale factor of 2 about centre (3, 2) to form image D. Draw triangle D.

  e Describe fully the transformation which maps T to B.

  f Describe fully the transformation which maps C to D.

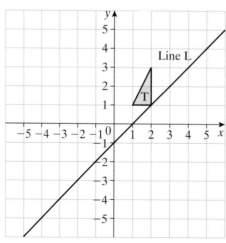

Distributions, quartiles, measures of spread and cumulative frequency

Exercise 25

For Questions 1–4, find the median, quartiles, range and interquartile range of the sets of numbers.

1 5, 6, 8, 1, 0, 7, 6

2 2, 5, 9, 0, 6, 1, 8, 1, 8, 6, 5, 0, 5, 5, 2

3 2, 11, 8, 5, 1, 3, 0, 6, 4

4 60, 83, 90, 59, 62, 83, 71, 46, 50, 82, 87, 21, 39

5 This frequency table shows how many detentions students in Mr. Tonge's class received last term. Find the median, quartiles, range and interquartile range of the number of detentions.

Number of detentions	Frequency
0	10
1	5
2	3
3	8
4	4
5	1

6 This frequency table gives the amount of time some students spent on the internet last night.

   a Construct a cumulative frequency table for the data.

   b Draw the cumulative frequency curve.

   c Use your curve to estimate the median, quartiles and interquartile range for the length of time spent on the internet.

   d How many students spent more than 32 minutes on the internet last night?

Time (t mins)	Frequency
$0 < t \leqslant 10$	3
$10 < t \leqslant 20$	7
$20 < t \leqslant 30$	15
$30 < t \leqslant 40$	27
$40 < t \leqslant 50$	19
$50 < t \leqslant 60$	9

7 The frequency table shows the results of a spot check of speeds of some cars on a motorway.

   a Construct a cumulative frequency table for the data.

   b Draw the cumulative frequency curve.

   c Use your curve to estimate the median, quartiles and interquartile range for the speeds of cars.

   d What percentage of cars were travelling at less than 63 m.p.h?

Speed (s m.p.h.)	Frequency
$s \leqslant 55$	0
$55 < s \leqslant 60$	6
$60 < s \leqslant 65$	19
$65 < s \leqslant 70$	46
$70 < s \leqslant 75$	14
$75 < s \leqslant 80$	5

8 The frequency table gives the birth weight of two
random samples of babies from different countries.

a Construct cumulative frequency tables for
the data.

b Draw the cumulative frequency curves on
one set of axes.

c Use your curves to estimate the median and
interquartile range of weights for both countries.

d Comment on the difference between the two
samples.

Weight (w kilograms)	Country A	Country B
w ⩽ 2.0	0	0
2.0 < w ⩽ 2.5	14	0
2.5 < w ⩽ 3.0	29	3
3.0 < w ⩽ 3.5	23	20
3.5 < w ⩽ 4.0	14	51
4.0 < w ⩽ 4.5	0	6

Exercise 25★

For Questions 1–4, find the median, quartiles, range and interquartile range of the sets of numbers.

1 4, 5, 5, 7, 8, 9, 0, 6, 8, 5, 9, 5, 4, 8, 7, 9, 3, 5, 8

2 5.1, 3.9, 9.0, 9.4, 0.9, 2.5, 4.6, 9.9, 1.8, 2.1, 2.9

3 39, 51, 32, 57, 77, 45, 70, 70, 89, 5, 83, 67, 77

4 0.21, 0.57, 0.58, 0.46, 0.91, 0.46, 0.78, 0.55

5 This frequency table shows how many books students in
Ms. Twitchitt's class read last term. Find the median, quartiles,
range and interquartile range of the number of books read.

Number of books	Frequency
0	6
1	8
2	11
3	5
4	2
5	1

6 The frequency table gives the amount of time some students
spent on their mobile phones last night.

a Construct a cumulative frequency table for the data.

b Draw the cumulative frequency curve.

c Use your curve to estimate the median, quartiles and
interquartile range for the amount of time spent on a
mobile phone.

d What percentage of students spent between 45 minutes
and 95 minutes on mobile phones last night?

Time (t mins)	Frequency
0 < t ⩽ 20	3
20 < t ⩽ 40	7
40 < t ⩽ 60	11
60 < t ⩽ 80	10
80 < t ⩽ 100	21
100 < t ⩽ 120	25
120 < t ⩽ 140	23

7 The frequency table gives the reaction times of a group of volunteers before and after drinking a can of fizzy drink.

a Construct cumulative frequency tables for the data.

b Draw the cumulative frequency curves on one set of axes.

c Use your curves to estimate the median and interquartile range for both reaction times.

d Comment on the difference the drink makes to reaction times.

Time (t milliseconds)	Frequency before drink	Frequency after drink
t ≤ 160	0	0
160 < t ≤ 180	10	0
180 < t ≤ 200	35	0
200 < t ≤ 220	31	8
220 < t ≤ 240	4	41
240 < t ≤ 260	0	25
260 < t ≤ 280	0	6

8 The frequency table gives the diameters of two random samples of tree trunks taken from two different woods, Short Wood and Waley Wood.

a Construct cumulative frequency tables for the data.

b Draw the cumulative frequency curves on one set of axes.

c Use your curves to estimate the median and interquartile range for the diameters of the tree trunks for both woods.

d Comment on the differences between the woods.

Diameter (d cm)	Frequency Short Wood	Frequency Waley Wood
0 < d ≤ 10	6	2
10 < d ≤ 20	9	3
20 < d ≤ 30	12	7
30 < d ≤ 40	23	38
40 < d ≤ 50	21	42
50 < d ≤ 60	14	6
60 < d ≤ 70	10	2
70 < d ≤ 80	5	0

1 Write these as a single power, and then calculate the answer correct to 3 significant figures.
   a $1.8^4 \times 1.8^5$ **b** $13.2^9 \div 13.2^3$ **c** $(1.24^3)^3$

2 To a scale of $1 : 500$, a garden is shown as 6 cm long. Find its actual length, in metres.

3 In 18 days, a queen termite lays 1 million eggs. How many eggs per minute is this?

4 **a** Convert 6 km into metres.
   b Convert 1 hour into seconds.
   c Hence convert 6 km/hour (walking speed) into metres per second.

5 The density of a flammable liquid is $0.8 \, \text{g/cm}^3$.
   a Find the mass, in grams, of 1 litre.
   b Find the mass, in kg, of $1 \, \text{m}^3$.

6 A 1.5 litre bottle of olive oil costs £6.99 at a local corner-shop. Given that 1 pint = 0.5682 litres, find the cost of one pint of olive oil.

7 When the fraction $\frac{1}{63}$ is written as a decimal, will it terminate or recur? Give a reason for your answer.

8 Expand and simplify these expressions.
   a $(x + 2)(x + 5)$ **b** $(y + 11)(y - 9)$ **c** $(3 - p)^2$

9 Expand and simplify these expressions.
   a $(5x - 3)(3x + 2)$ **b** $(a - 3b)^2$

10 Factorise these expressions.
   a $x^2 - 3x$ **b** $x^2 - 49$
   c $x^2 + 3x + 2$ **d** $x^2 - 7x - 8$

11 Factorise these completely.
   a $x^2 - 10x + 21$ **b** $3p^4 - 12p^2$

12 Solve these quadratic equations by factorising.
   a $x^2 + 7x + 12 = 0$ **b** $x^2 - x - 6 = 0$
   c $x^2 - 3x = 0$ **d** $x^2 = 12x - 20$

13 **a** Factorise $a^2 - ab$.
   b Using factors, calculate the **exact** value of $987654321^2 - 987654321 \times 987654320$

14 For each sequence, find

   i the next two terms   **ii** a formula for the nth term   **iii** the value of the 55th term.

   a 3, 10, 17, 24, 31, …   **b** 30, 26, 22, 18, …

15 Josie invested £450 at simple interest at a rate of 3.8% per annum. She earned £51.30 interest in total. For how many years did Josie invest the £450?

16 a Use Pythagoras' theorem to form an equation in x for this right-angled triangle.

   b Solve your equation to find x.

17 The width of a rectangle is x cm. The length is 5 cm more than the width, and the area is 36 cm^2.

   a Form an equation in x.

   b Solve your equation to find the dimensions of the rectangle.

   c Find the size of the acute angle between the diagonals of the rectangle. Give your answer to the nearest tenth of a degree.

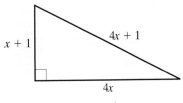

18 a On graph paper draw x and y-axes such that $0 \leqslant x \leqslant 16$ and $0 \leqslant y \leqslant 16$.

   b Draw and label the square A with corners at $(0, 2)$, $(2, 2)$, $(2, 4)$ and $(0, 4)$.

   c Draw and label the square B with corners at $(10, 12)$, $(12, 12)$, $(12, 14)$ and $(10, 14)$.

   d What translation transforms A to B?

A reflection in the line L transforms A to B.

   e Draw and label the line L on your diagram. Give the equation of the line L.

A rotation with centre $(6, 8)$ transforms A to B.

   f State the angle of this rotation.

A 90° clockwise rotation with centre C transforms A to B.

   g What are the coordinates of C? Label the point C on your diagram.

An enlargement with centre $(0, 0)$ and scale factor 3 transforms A to E, then another enlargement transforms E to B.

   h Draw the square E on your diagram.

   i Find the coordinates of the centre, and the scale factor, of the second enlargement.

19 The table shows the number of phone calls that Tina made each day in June. Find the median, quartiles, range and interquartile range of the number of phone calls made each day.

16	25	18	39	31	13
35	15	38	17	27	11
19	23	31	18	23	29
14	22	34	21	33	30
35	25	29	17	24	21

20 The frequency table shows the weights of some chocolate bars in a presentation box.

  a How many chocolate bars are in the box?

  b Construct a cumulative frequency table for the data.

  c Draw the cumulative frequency curve.

  d Use your curve to obtain estimates of the median weight and the quartiles.

  e Work out the inter-quartile range.

  f What percentage of bars weigh more than 75 grams?

Weight (w g)	Frequency
$66 < w \leqslant 68$	5
$68 < w \leqslant 70$	13
$70 < w \leqslant 72$	18
$72 < w \leqslant 74$	10
$74 < w \leqslant 76$	8
$76 < w \leqslant 78$	6